DEPARTMENT OF THE NAVY
HEADQUARTERS UNITED STATES MARINE CORPS
3000 MARINE CORPS PENTAGON
WASHINGTON, DC 20350-3000

I0415695

UC-12W T&R MANUAL

DEPARTMENT OF THE NAVY
HEADQUARTERS UNITED STATES MARINE CORPS
3000 MARINE CORPS PENTAGON
WASHINGTON, DC 20350-3000

NAVMC 3500.102
C4610

OCT 1 3 2010

NAVMC 3500.102

From: Commandant of the Marine Corps
To: Distribution List

Subj: UC-12W T&R MANUAL

Ref: (a) NAVMC 3500.14B

Encl: (1) UC-12W T&R MANUAL

1. Purpose. To publish standards and regulations regarding the training of UC-12W aircrew per the reference.

2. Information. Highlights of major training and readiness planning considerations included in this, the first UC-12W T&R Manual, are as follows:

    a. Establishment of Mission Essential Task List (METL) TO facilitate MET-based readiness.

    b. Incorporation of Marine Corps Task (MCT) list.

    c. Emphasis on Mission Skills to support MET-based reporting.

    d. Inclusion of Aviation Career Progression Model (ACPM) training requirements.

3. Recommendations. Recommended changes to this Manual are invited, and may be submitted via the syllabus sponsor and the appropriate chain of command to: Commanding General, Training and Education Command, Aviation Training Division using standard Naval correspondence or the Automated Message Handling System plain language address: CG TECOM ATB.

4. Reserve Applicability. This Manual is applicable to the Marine Corps Total Force.

5. Certification. Reviewed and approved this date.

R. C. FOX
By direction

DISTRIBUTION: PCN 10031982200

CHAPTER 1

UC-12W TRAINING AND READINESS UNIT REQUIREMENTS

CHAPTER 1

UC-12W

100. <u>MARINE OPERATIONAL SUPPORT AIRCRAFT (OSA) SQUADRONS AND DETACHMENTS (VMR Det. UC-12W) UNIT TRAINING AND READINESS REQUIREMENTS</u>. The goal of Marine Aviation is to attain and maintain combat readiness to support Expeditionary Maneuver Warfare while conserving resources. The standards established in this program are validated by subject matter experts to maximize combat capabilities for assigned METs. These standards describe and define unit capabilities and requirements necessary to maintain proficiency in mission skills and combat leadership. Training events are based on specific requirements and performance standards to ensure a common base of training and depth of combat capability.

101. <u>OSA/UC-12W MISSION</u>. Provide time-sensitive air transport of high priority passengers and cargo to, within, and between theaters of war.

102. <u>TABLE OF ORGANIZATION (T/O)</u>. As of this publication date, UC-12W VMR Dets for both the Active and Reserve Forces are authorized:

Table of Organization Active Forces		
VMR Det MCAS Futenma	VMR Det MCAS Miramar	VMR Det MCAS Iwakuni
T/O # M02204	T/O # M02209	T/O # M02204
1 UC-12W	1 UC-12W	2 UC-12W
Pilots*	Pilots*	Pilots*
10	12	10
Transport Aircrewman	Transport Aircrewman	Transport Aircrewman
3	3	3
Table of Organization Reserve Forces		
VMR Det JRB Belle Chase		
T/O M03017		
2 UC-12W		
Pilots*		
21		
Transport Aircrewman		
3		
Table of Organization (Deployed Detachment)		
2 UC-12W	1 UC-12	
Pilots*	Pilots*	
7	5	
Transport Aircrewman	Transport Aircrewman	
3**	2**	
*A Qualified Observer may be counted as a T2P on certain events.		
**The Transport Aircrewman is not required on all Mission Flights		

103. CORE SKILLS AND MISSION SKILL ABBREVIATIONS. Shading indicates Core Plus Skills.

CORE SKILLS	
FSI	FLIGHT SAFETY INTERNATIONAL
CACT	COMMAND AIRCRAFT CREW TRAINING
FAM	FAMILIARIZATION
NFAM	NIGHT FAMILIARIZATION
INST	INSTRUMENT
CP	CO-PILOT PROCEDURES
MISSION SKILLS	
OSA	OPERATIONAL SUPPORT AIRLIFT
ALS	AIR LOGISTICS SUPPORT
CORE PLUS SKILLS	
INT	INTERNATIONAL PROCEDURES
MISSION PLUS	
AS	ASSAULT SUPPORT
EXP	EXPEDITIONARY SHORE-BASED OPERATIONS

104. CORE METL AND CORE METL OUTPUT STANDARDS

1. Core METL. A list of specified tasks that VMR-1 and VMR Dets are designed to perform.

Core METL

MCT 1.3.4.1.2	Conduct Operational Support Airlift
MCT 4.3.8	Conduct Air Logistics Support

Core Plus

MCT 1.3.4	Conduct Assault Support Operations
MCT 1.3.3.3.2	Conduct Aviation Operations From Expeditionary Shore-Based Sites

2. VMR Det. The required level of performance that a VMR Det must be capable of sustaining to be considered MET-Ready.

VMR Det (UC-12W)				
Core METL Output Standards (2/1 A/C)				
MCT	MET	MAXIMUM DAILY SORTIES	MAXIMUM SORTIES PER MET	CMMR
MCT 1.3.4.1.2 OSA	Conduct Operational Support Airlift	5/3	5/3	3/2
MCT 4.3.8 ALS	Conduct Air Logistics Support		5/3	3/2
Core Plus METL Output Standards				
MCT	MET	MAXIMUM DAILY SORTIES	MAXIMUM SORTIES PER MET	CMMR
MCT 1.3.4 AS	Conduct Assault Support Operations	5/3	5/3	3/2
MCT 1.3.3.3.2 EXP	Conduct Aviation Operations From Expeditionary Shore-Based Sites		5/3	3/2

Note: VMR Det (UC-12W) (2/1 A/C) is able to execute 5/3 total overall sorties on a daily (24 hour period) basis. Based on historical flight hour data, average sortie duration is 3.0 hours for the UC-12W.

3. VMR Deployed Detachment. The required level of performance that VMR-1 or a VMR Det must be capable of sustaining during deployed contingency operations to be considered MET-ready.

VMR Deployed Detachment (UC-12W)				
Core METL Output Standards (2/1 A/C Det)				
MCT	MET	MAXIMUM DAILY SORTIES	MAXIMUM SORTIES PER MET	CMMR
MCT 1.3.4.1.2 OSA	Conduct Operational Support Airlift	5/3	5/3	3/2
MCT 4.3.8 ALS	Conduct Air Logistics Support		5/3	3/2
Core Plus METL Output Standards				
MCT	MET	MAXIMUM DAILY SORTIES	MAXIMUM SORTIES PER MET	CMMR
MCT 1.3.4 AS	Conduct Assault Support Operations	5/3	5/3	3/2
MCT 1.3.3.3.2 EXP	Conduct Aviation Operations From Expeditionary Shore-Based Sites		5/3	3/2

Note: A VMR UC-12W Deployed Detachment (2/1 A/C) is able to execute 5/3 total overall sorties on a daily (24 hour period) basis during contingency/combat operations. Based on historical flight hour data, average sortie duration is 3.0 hours for the UC-12W.

105. CORE MCT TO CORE/MISSION/CORE PLUS SKILL MATRIX. Provides a pictorial view of the relationship between the Core MCT (Marine Corps Task) and each Core/Mission/Core Plus skill required to perform the MCT. Shading indicates a Core Plus.

UC-12W										
Mission Essential Task To Core/Mission/Core Plus Skill Matrix										
MISSION ESSENTIAL TASK (MET) // MARINE CORPS TASK (MCT)	CORE SKILLS 2000 PHASE					MISSION SKILLS 3000 PHASE		CORE PLUS 4000 PHASE		
								SKILL	MISSION	
	FAM	INST	NFAM	CP	FAM REV	OSA	ALS	INT	AS	EXE
MCT 1.3.4.1.2 Conduct Operational Support Airlift OSA	X	X	X	X	X	X				
MCT 4.3.8 Conduct Air Logistics Support ALS	X	X	X	X	X		X			
MCT 1.3.4 Conduct Assault Support Operations AS	X	X	X	X	X			X	X	
MCT 1.3.3.3.2 Conduct Aviation Operations From Expeditionary Shore-Based Sites EXP	X	X	X							X

106. CMMR CORE/MISSION/CORE PLUS SKILLS CREW DEFINITION AND PROFICIENCY REQUIREMENTS

a. VMR Det. This table delineates crew position and proficiency requirements for each Core/Mission/Core Plus Skill. The numbers associated with each crew position column reflect the number of Core/Mission/Core Plus Skill proficient individuals required.

VMR Det (UC-12W)			
CMMR (2/1 A/C)			
CORE SKILLS (2000 Phase)			
CORE SKILL	PILOTS	TRANSPORT AIRCREWMAN	CREWS
FAM	7/5	3/2**	3/2
INST	7/5	N/A	3/2
NFAM	7/5	N/A	3/2
CP	7/5	N/A	3/2
FAM REV	7/5	N/A	3/2
MISSION SKILLS (3000 Phase)			
MISSION SKILL	PILOTS	TRANSPORT AIRCREWMAN**	CREWS
OSA	7/5*	3/2**	3/2
ALS	7/5*	3/2**	3/2
CORE PLUS (4000 Phase)			
CORE PLUS SKILL	PILOTS	TRANSPORT AIRCREWMAN	CREWS
INT	7/5*	3/2**	3/2
MISSION PLUS	PILOTS	TRANSPORT AIRCREWMAN	CREWS
AS	7/5*	3/2**	3/2
EXP	7/5*	3/2**	3/2
*Note: A Qualified Observer may fill duties of T2P on selected flights			
**The Transport Aircrewman is not required on all Mission Flights			

b. VMR Deployed Detachment. This table delineates crew position and proficiency requirements for each Core/Mission/Core Plus Skill. The numbers associated with each crew position column reflect the number of Core/Mission/Core Plus Skill proficient individuals required.

VMR Deployed Detachment(UC-12W)			
CMMR (2/1 A/C)			
CORE SKILLS (2000 Phase)			
CORE SKILL	PILOTS	TRANSPORT AIRCREWMAN	CREWS
FAM	7/5	3/2*	3/2
INST	7/5	N/A	3/2
NFAM	7/5	N/A	3/2
CP	7/5	N/A	3/2
FAM REV	7/5	N/A	3/2
MISSION SKILLS (3000 Phase)			
MISSION SKILL	PILOTS	TRANSPORT AIRCREWMAN	CREWS
OSA	7/5*	3/2*	3/2
ALS	7/5*	3/2*	3/2
CORE PLUS (4000 Phase)			
CORE PLUS SKILL	PILOTS	TRANSPORT AIRCREWMAN	CREWS
INT	7/5*	2/2*	2/2
MISSION PLUS	PILOTS	TRANSPORT AIRCREWMAN	CREWS
AS	7/5*	2/2*	2/2
EXP	7/5*	2/2*	2/2
*Note: A Qualified Observer may fill duties of T2P on selected flights			
*The Transport Aircrewman is not required on all Mission Flights			

107. INSTRUCTOR REQUIREMENTS

a. VMR Det. A VMR Det should possess the following numbers of personnel with the instructor designations listed in the matrix.

VMR-1 or VMR Det (UC-12W) CMMR (2/1 A/C)		
INSTRUCTOR DESIGNATIONS (5000 PHASE)		
DESIGNATIONS	PILOTS	TRANSPORT AIRCREWMAN
ANI (Assistant NATOPS Inst)	3/2	N/A
NI (NATOPS Instructor)	1/1	1/1
Instrument Evaluator	3/2	N/A
Transport Aircrewman Instructor	N/A	3/2

b. **VMR Deployed Detachment**. A deployed VMR Det should possess the following numbers of personnel with the instructor designations listed in the matrix.

VMR Deployed Det (UC-12W) CMMR (2/1 A/C)		
INSTRUCTOR DESIGNATIONS (5000 PHASE)		
DESIGNATIONS	PILOTS	TRANSPORT AIRCREWMAN
ANI (Assistant NATOPS Inst)	2/1	N/A
NI (NATOPS Instructor)	1/1	1/1
Instrument Evaluator	1/1	N/A
Transport Aircrewman Instructor	N/A	1/1

108. CMMR FLIGHT LEADERSHIP REQUIREMENTS

a. **VMR Det**. A VMR Det to be considered Core Competent, must possess the following numbers of crews with the listed flight leadership designations.

VMR-1 or VMR Det (UC-12W) CMMR (2/1 A/C)		
FLIGHT LEADERSHIP (6000 PHASE)		
DESIGNATION	PILOTS	TRANSPORT AIRCREWMAN
T2P*	3/2	N/A
TAC	7/5	N/A
TRANSPORT AIRCREWMAN	N/A	3/2
FCF	3/2	N/A
*A Qualified Observer may perform duties of T2P on selected missions.		

b. **VMR Deployed Detachment**. A deployed VMR Detachment should possess the following numbers of personnel with the flight leadership designations.

VMR Deployed Det (UC-12W) CMMR (2/1 A/C)		
FLIGHT LEADERSHIP (6000 PHASE)		
DESIGNATION	PILOTS	TRANSPORT AIRCREWMAN
T2P*	2/1	N/A
TAC	5/4	N/A
TRANSPORT AIRCREWMAN	N/A	2/1
FCF	2/1	N/A
*A Qualified Observer may perform duties of T2P on selected missions.		

CHAPTER 2

UC-12W PILOT/7555

CHAPTER 2

UC-12W PILOT/7555

200. <u>UC-12W PILOT/7555 INDIVIDUAL TRAINING AND READINESS REQUIREMENTS</u>. This
T&R syllabus is based on specific goals and performance standards designed to
ensure individual proficiency in Core, Mission and Core Plus Skills. The goal
of this chapter is to develop individual and unit war fighting capabilities.

201. <u>UC-12W PILOT TRAINING PROGRESSION MODEL</u>. This model represents the
recommended training progression for the average UC-12W pilot crewmember.
Units should use the model as a guide to generate individual training plans.

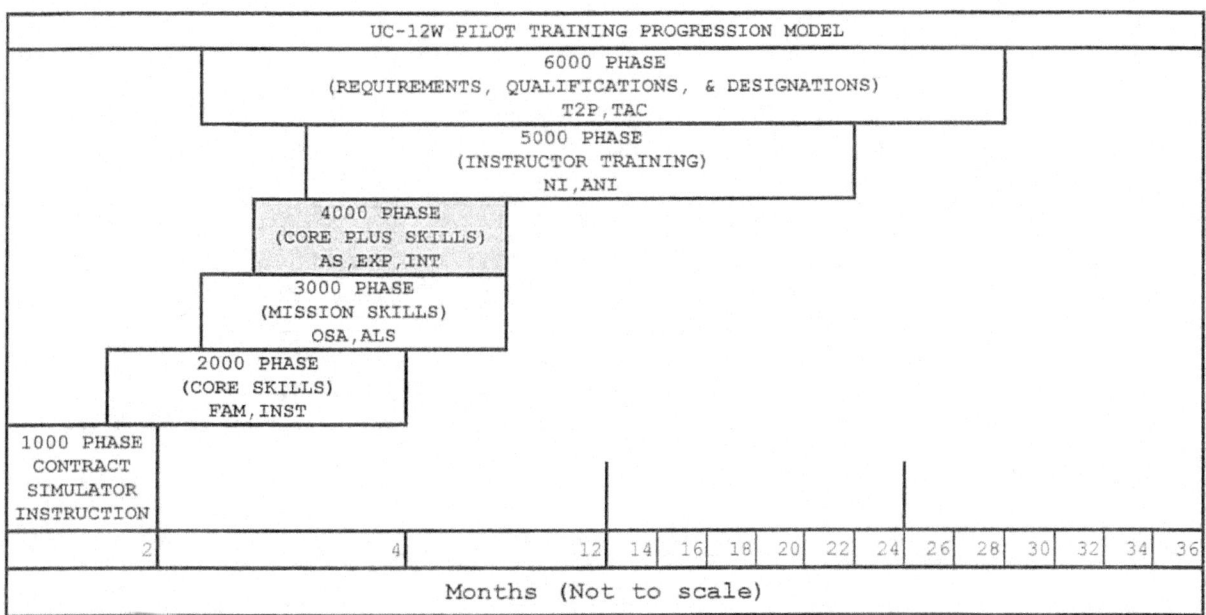

202. <u>INDIVIDUAL CORE SKILL PROFICIENCY (CSP) REQUIREMENTS</u>. A CSP crew
consists of individuals representing each crew position who have achieved and
currently maintain individual CSP. In order to be considered proficient in a
Core Skill, an individual must attain and maintain proficiency in Core Skill
events as delineated in the below paragraphs.

1. <u>Events Required to Attain Individual CSP</u>. To initially attain CSP in a
Core Skill, an individual must simultaneously have a proficient status in all
of the Core (2000 Phase) T&R events listed in the table below for that Core
Skill.

INDIVIDUAL CORE SKILL PROFICIENCY (CSP) ATTAIN TABLE UC-12W Pilot				
T&R events required to Attain CSP (2000 Phase)				
FAM	INST	NFAM	CP	FAM REV
2100 2101R	2200R 2201R	2300R	2400 2401R	2500
Gray highlight & an R suffix on the event code = Refresher POI				
An S prefix on the event code = Event conducted in a simulator				

2. Events Required to Maintain Individual CSP. To maintain CSP in a Core Skill, an individual must maintain proficiency in all 2000 phase T&R events listed for that Core Skill:

INDIVIDUAL CORE SKILL PROFICIENCY (CSP) MAINTAIN TABLE UC-12W Pilot				
T&R events required to Maintain CSP (2000 Phase)				
FAM	INST	NFAM	CP	FAM REV
2101R	2201R	2300R	2401R	
Gray highlight & an R suffix on the event code = Refresher POI				
An S prefix on the event code = Event conducted in a simulator				

203. INDIVIDUAL MISSION SKILL PROFICIENCY (MSP) REQUIREMENTS. A MSP crew consists of individuals representing each crew position who have achieved and currently maintain Individual MSP. To be considered proficient in a Mission Skill, an individual must attain and maintain proficiency in Mission Skill events as delineated in the below paragraphs.

1. Events Required to Attain Individual MSP. To initially attain MSP in a Mission Skill, an individual must simultaneously have a proficient status in all 3000 phase T&R events listed for that Mission Skill:

INDIVIDUAL MISSION SKILL PROFICIENCY (MSP) ATTAIN TABLE UC-12W Pilot	
T&R events required to Attain MSP (3000 Phase)	
OSA	ALS
3100R	3200R
Gray highlight & an R suffix on the event code = Refresher POI	
An S prefix on the event code = Event conducted in a simulator	

2. Events Required to Maintain Individual MSP. To maintain MSP in a Mission Skill, an individual must maintain proficiency in all 3000 phase T&R events listed for that Mission Skill:

INDIVIDUAL MISSION SKILL PROFICIENCY (MSP) MAINTAIN TABLE UC-12W Pilot	
T&R events required to Maintain MSP (3000 Phase)	
OSA	ALS
3100R	3200R
Gray highlight & an R suffix on the event code = Refresher POI	
An S prefix on the event code = Event conducted in a simulator	

204. INDIVIDUAL CORE PLUS SKILL/MISSION PLUS SKILL PROFICIENCY REQUIREMENTS

1. Events Required to Attain Individual Proficiency in Core Plus Skills and Mission Plus Skills. Proficiency in Core Plus Skills/Mission Plus Skills is not required to obtain unit CSP. Training to Core Plus Skills/Mission Plus Skills is at the discretion of the unit commanding officer. To initially attain proficiency in a Core Plus Skill/Mission Plus Skill, an individual must simultaneously have a proficient status in all T&R events listed for that Core Plus Skill/Mission Plus Skill.

INDIVIDUAL CORE PLUS SKILL PROFICIENCY ATTAIN TABLE UC-12W Pilot			
T&R events required to Attain Core Plus Proficiency (4000 Phase)			
CORE PLUS MISSION			CORE PLUS SKILL
AS	EXP		INT
4100R	4200R		4300R
			4301R
Gray highlight & an R suffix on the event code = Refresher POI			
An S prefix on the event code = Event conducted in a simulator			

2. <u>Events Required to Maintain Individual Proficiency in Core Plus Skills and Mission Plus Skills</u>. To maintain proficiency in a Core Plus Skill/Mission Plus Skill, an individual must maintain proficiency in all T&R events listed in the table below for that Core Plus Skill Mission Plus Skill:

INDIVIDUAL CORE PLUS SKILL PROFICIENCY MAINTAIN TABLE UC-12W Pilot		
T&R events required to Maintain Core Plus Proficiency (4000 Phase)		
CORE PLUS MISSION		CORE PLUS SKILL
AS	EXP	INT
4100R	4200R	4300R
		4301R
Gray highlight & an R suffix on the event code = Refresher POI		
An S prefix on the event code = Event conducted in a simulator		

205. <u>CERTIFICATION, QUALIFICATION AND DESIGNATION TABLES</u>. The tables below delineate T&R events required to be completed to attain proficiency, initial qualifications and designations. In addition to event requirements, all required stage lectures, briefs, squadron training, prerequisites, and other criteria shall be completed prior to completing final events. Certification, qualification and designation letters signed by the commanding officer shall be placed in Aircrew Performance Records (APR) and NATOPS. Loss of proficiency in all qualification events causes the associated qualification to be lost. Regaining a qualification requires completing all R-coded syllabus events associated with that qualification.

INDIVIDUAL DESIGNATION REQUIREMENTS UC-12W Pilot	
Designation	Initial Event Designation Requirements
ANI	5100,5101,5102,5103
NI	5100,5101,5102,5103
T2P	6300
TAC	6400,6401,6402
FCF	6500,6501,6008

INDIVIDUAL QUALIFICATION REQUIREMENTS UC-12W Pilot	
Qualification	Initial Event Qualification Requirements
NATOPS	6000,6001,6002,6100
STANDARD INSTRUMENT	6003,6004,6005,6101
SPECIAL INSTRUMENT	6003,6004,6005,6102
CRM	6006,6007

206. <u>PROGRAMS OF INSTRUCTION (POI)</u>

1. <u>General</u>. Those aviators with less than 200 military fixed-wing hours shall be assigned to the Basic (B) POI. Those aviators with more than 200 military fixed-wing hours will be assigned to the Refresher (R) POI. Those aviators that have been previously designated a UC-12W TAC and are returning to a DIFOP status should be assigned to the Refresher(R) POI. Final determination of a training track for a pilot will be at the discretion of the individual command. When a crewmember completes a stage of training, that crewmember need only maintain proficiency in the R coded events for that stage to remain proficient.

2. <u>Basic (B) POI</u>. Basic Pilots shall fly the entire syllabus.

WEEKS	COURSE	PERFORMING ACTIVITY
1-8	Core Skill Introduction Training	CACT
9-16	Core Skill Training	VMR Det
16-52	Mission Skill Training	VMR Det
16-52	Core Plus Training	VMR Det

3. <u>Refresher (R) POI</u>. Refresher Pilots shall fly those events annotated with an R. Commanding officers/OICs will review the qualifications, previous experience, currency, and demonstrated ability of Refresher Pilots with a view towards combining required flights.

WEEKS	COURSE	PERFORMING ACTIVITY
1-8	Core Skill Introduction Training	CACT
9-12	Core Skill Training	VMR Det
13-26	Mission Skill Training	VMR Det
13-26	Core Plus Training	VMR Det

207. <u>CORE SKILL INTRODUCTION (1000 PHASE)</u>

1. <u>General</u>

   a. Core Skill Introduction training for the UC-12W is conducted by a Command Aircraft Crew Training (CACT) facility. The UC-12W Syllabus Sponsor is responsible for contract negotiations and syllabus content/changes. Recommendations for CACT changes shall be submitted to the Syllabus Sponsor.

   b. All academic requirements for this phase of training are incorporated into the CACT course.

   c. All events in the Core Skill Introduction phase shall be evaluated and documented by a civilian instructor. The Syllabus Sponsor shall ensure standardization of civilian contracted instructors.

   d. Event completion is predicated upon demonstrated proficiency. When an individual successfully accomplishes the requirements of an event per the performance standards, the individual should log completion of the event (enter the appropriate T&R code) in M-SHARP. When the event is entered into M-SHARP, the individual's proficiency date for that event is automatically updated to reflect the date the event was completed. When supervising individual events, unit instructors/leaders shall ensure that trainees demonstrate proficiency per T&R standards prior to logging successful event completion. Evaluating individual proficiency in an event normally requires both objective and subjective assessment. If an individual fails to accomplish the requirements of an event per the performance standards, the individual should not log that event and the proficiency status for that event remains unchanged. Times indicated for each event are for planning purposes only.

   e. Pilots shall fly events annotated with an N at least 30 minutes after official sunset. Events shall be flown in accordance with environmental conditions listed in the matrix below:

ENVIRONMENTAL CONDITIONS	
Code	Meaning
D	Shall be flown during hours of daylight: (by exception - there is no use of a symbol)
N*	Shall be flown during hours of darkness must be flown unaided
(N*)	May be flown during hours of darkness - If flown during hours of darkness must be flown unaided
Note - If the event is to be flown in the simulator the Simulator Instructor shall set the desired environmental conditions for the event.	

2. Command Aircraft Crew Training (CACT) Ground School

ACAD-1000   48.0   *   B   CLRM

> Goal. CACT Initial Ground School: Aircraft Systems, CRM, Weight & Balance, Performance, flight planning, Windshear, TAWS/CFIT, TCASII.
>
> Requirements. Per current contract.
>
> Performance Standard. Per current contract.

ACAD-1001   8.0   365   R   CLRM

> Goal. CACT Recurrent Ground School.
>
> Requirements. Per current contract.
>
> Performance Standard. Per current contract.
>
> Prerequisite. ACAD-1000

ACAD-1002   3.0   *   B   CLRM

> Goal. RVSM.
>
> Requirements. Per current contract.
>
> Performance Standard. Per current contract.

ACAD-1003   2.0   365   B,R   CLRM

> Goal. Weather Radar.
>
> Requirements. Per current contract.
>
> Performance Standard. Per current contract.

ACAD-1004   21.0   *   B,R   CLRM

> Goal. CACT Initial International Procedures
>
> Requirements. Per current contract.
>
> Performance Standard. Per current contract.

ACAD-1005   8.0   730   R   CLRM

> Goal. CACT Recurrent International Procedures
>
> Requirements. Per current contract.

Performance Standard. Per current contract.

Prerequisite. ACAD-1004

4. Command Aircraft Crew Training (CACT) Simulator Training

CACT-1101   4.0   *   B   (N*)   S

    Goal. Per current contract.

    Requirements. Per current contract.

    Performance Standard. Per current contract.

CACT-1102   4.0   *   B   (N*)   S

    Goal. Per current contract.

    Requirements. Per current contract.

    Performance Standard. Per current contract.

CACT-1103   4.0   *   B   (N*)   S

    Goal. Per current contract.

    Requirements. Per current contract.

    Performance Standard. Per current contract.

CACT-1104   4.0   *   B   (N*)   S

    Goal. Per current contract.

    Requirements. Per current contract.

    Performance Standard. Per current contract.

CACT-1105   4.0   365   B,R   (N*)   S

    Goal. Per current contract.

    Requirements. Per current contract.

    Performance Standard. Per current contract.

CACT-1106   4.0   365   B,R   (N*)   S

    Goal. Per current contract.

    Requirements. Per current contract.

    Performance Standard. Per current contract.

CACT-1107   4.0   365   B,R   (N*)   S

    Goal. Per current contract.

    Requirements. Per current contract.

    Performance Standard. Per current contract.

208. CORE SKILL (2000 PHASE)

1. Core Skill Academic (ACAD)

   a. Purpose. Introduce the Pilots to the UC-12W.

b. <u>General</u>. The Pilot should be CACT complete prior to beginning this stage.

ACAD-2000   3.0   *   B,R   D   A   1 UC-12W (Static)

> <u>Goal</u>. Introduce the UC-12W aircraft.
>
> <u>Requirements</u>
>
> Brief: ADB, MEL/CDL, Chapter 29 Flight Crew Coordination, Pre-flight, Emergency Equipment, Egress Drill, Post Flight, M-Sharp, CP-CALC, Flight-planning, ORM, WX Brief, NOTAMS, Fuel Packet/Multi-use Card, OPARS, Short Field High Obstacle. Discuss engine failure during critical phases of flight. Discuss Rapid depressurization and Time of Useful Consciousness. Discuss dual engine failure. Discuss Ditching with two engines, single engine, and power off.
>
> <u>Performance Standard</u>. After introduction of above listed items, demonstrate understanding of each subject.
>
> <u>External Syllabus Support</u>. Static aircraft.
>
> <u>Prerequisite</u>. 1000, 1001, 1101-1107

ACAD-2001   3.0   *   B,R   D   A   1 UC-12W (Static)

> <u>Goal</u>. Introduce the UC-12W avionics and navigation systems on a powered aircraft.
>
> <u>Requirements</u>. Demonstrate the power up, set up, and various functions of the FMS, radios and avionics.
>
> <u>Performance Standard</u>. Show proficiency in the use of all navigation equipment and radios.
>
> <u>External Syllabus Support</u>. Ground powered aircraft.
>
> <u>Prerequisite</u>. 2000

2. <u>Familiarization (FAM)</u>

a. <u>Purpose</u>. Introduce Pilots to UC-12W FAM and CRM procedures. Develop proficiency as a T2P with the aircraft in all takeoff, landing, and flight modes. At the completion of the core skill basic pase the PUI should be able to meet performance standards for various maneuvers IAW the UC-12W NATOPS manual.

b. <u>General</u>

(1) This phase contains basic core skill training essential to operational employment of the UC-12W. Basic and Refresher Pilots shall be trained and evaluated in the appropriate seat.

(2) At the completion of this phase of training, and the T2P 6200 event, the PUI should be designated a Transport Second Pilot (T2P).

(3) Basic and Refresher Pilots shall complete the CACT prior to commencing flight training.

(4) The Core Skill Phase shall be conducted at the OSA unit/VMR Det.

(5) Flights in this stage of instruction shall be flown with a designated IP, and include a complete brief/debrief for each flight.

c. <u>Crew Requirements</u>. IP and PUI. An NI/ANI shall instruct the PUI for all initial flights.

FAM-2100   2.0   *   B   D   A   1 UC-12W

Goal. Introduce the pilot to preflight and ground checklist procedures for UC-12W aircraft.

Requirements

Brief: Stall warning, aircraft handling, Take-off abort, landing profile/landing techniques, engine limitations, electrical limitations, airframe limitations.

Flight: Practice: Start, taxi, take off, climbs/descents, steep turns, slow flight, stabilized approach, landing, Crew Resource Management.

Performance Standard. Demonstrate safe and proficient air work and show the ability to recognize deviation from Airline Transport Pilot (ATP) Practical Test Standards (PTS) standards and work towards correction. Operate the aircraft according to the NFM, IFM, and FARs.

Prerequisite. 2000, 2001

FAM-2101   2.0   365   B,R   D   A   1 UC-12W

Goal. Introduce expanded flight envelope.

Requirements

Brief: Aborted takeoffs, Short Field/High Obstacles, Go-around crew coordination, powerplant malfunctions prior to/at V1, engine failures during critical phases of flight, crosswind landing techniques, aerodynamic/fuel/autopilot limitations. Discuss emergency evacuation of passengers and crew, review emergency evacuation procedures.

Flight: Practice- Simulated Single-Engine Failure on Takeoff (NATOPS), Approach to Stall, Emergency Descent, Approach and Landing, Two-Engine Go-Around, Single-engine Go-Around, and Reduced Flap Landings (0/15)

Performance Standard. Demonstrate safe and proficient air work and show the ability to recognize deviation from Airline Transport Pilot (ATP) Practical Test Standards (PTS) standards and work towards correction. Operate the aircraft according to the NFM, IFM and FARs.

External Syllabus Support. Approved working area or restricted area.

Prerequisite. 2100

3. Instruments (INST)

a. Purpose. Introduce Pilots to UC-12W Instrument procedures under actual or simulated instrument flying conditions. PUI should demonstrate keen awareness of flight instrument interpretation and spatial orientation.

b. General. Basic and Refresher Pilots shall be trained and evaluated in the left seat. One of the instrument flights should be flown at night.

c. Crew Requirements. PUI shall be instructed/evaluated by an NI/ANI.

INST-2200   2.0   *   B,R   (N*)   A   1 UC-12W

Goal. Introduce instrument flying in the UC-12W.

Requirements

Brief: Set-up of FMS,MFD,PFD. Discuss Jeppeson approach plates, NAVFIG, Giant Report, TCASII warnings & conflict resolution maneuvers, IFR minimums.

Flight: ILS (coupled/non-coupled), PAR, Standby Gyro approach, Go-around, VOR holding, FMS holding.

Performance Standard. Demonstrate safe and proficient air work and show the ability to recognize deviation from Airline Transport Pilot (ATP) Practical Test Standards (PTS) standards and work towards correction. Operate the aircraft according to the NFM, IFM and FARs. Demonstrate sound Crew Resource Management (CRM).

Prerequisite. 2101

INST-2201   2.0   365   B,R   (N*)   A   1 UC-12W

Goal. Introduce expanded instrument flight and high altitude operations.

Requirements

Brief: RNAV/GPS, LNAV/MDA, LNAV/VNAV, VOR/TAC, ASR, B/C, GPS HOLDING, Instrument missed approach procedures, Standby Gyro Approach, NDB. Discuss volcanic ash hazards, recognition, avoidance. Review pressurization system, rapid decompression, door open warning annunciation procedures in flight, emergency descent procedures.

Flight: RNAV/GPS, LNAV/MDA, LNAV/VNAV, VOR/TAC, ASR, GPS holding, Instrument missed approach procedures, Standby Gyro Approach

Performance Standard. Demonstrate safe and proficient air work and show the ability to recognize deviation from Airline Transport Pilot (ATP) Practical Test Standards (PTS) standards and work towards correction. Operate the aircraft according to the NFM, IFM and FARs. Demonstrate sound Crew Resource Management (CRM).

Prerequisite. 2101

4. Night Familiarization (NFAM)

a. Purpose. Introduce Pilots to UC-12W Night Familiarization procedures.

b. General. Basic, Conversion, and Refresher Pilots shall be trained and evaluated in the left seat.

c. Crew Requirements. Shall be instructed/evaluated by an NI/ANI.

NFAM-2300   1.5   180   B,R   N*   A   1 UC-12W

Goal. Introduce night flying in the UC-12W.

Requirements

Brief: Cockpit management and lighting, night emergency procedures to include; electrical fire and electrical failure, emergency lighting pack, and visual illusions. Discuss Terrain Awareness Warning System (TAWS), Controlled Flight into Terrain (CFIT) hazards and recognition, CFIT escape maneuver.

Flight: Landing pattern, instrument approaches, simulated single engine failures, and go-around (one and two engines).

Performance Standard. Demonstrate safe and proficient air work and show the ability to recognize deviation from Airline Transport Pilot (ATP) Practical Test Standards (PTS) standards and work towards correction. Operate the aircraft according to the NFM, IFM and FARs. Demonstrate sound Crew Resource Management (CRM).

Prerequisite. 2101

5. Co-Pilot Responsibility (CP)

    a. Purpose. Introduce UC-12W Co-Pilot responsibilities.

    b. General. Basic and Refresher Pilots shall be trained and evaluated in the right seat.

    c. Crew Requirements. PUI shall be instructed/evaluated by an NI/ANI.

CP-2400   2.0   *   B   (N*)   A   1 UC-12W

Goal. Introduce right seat (pilot not flying) navigation, communication, and cockpit management duties. Introduce right seat approaches and landings.

Requirements

Brief: Aircraft servicing, NATOPS - Chapter 29 Flight Crew Coordination, ditching, weather radar, satellite phone, cabin ICS and audio capabilities, passenger/environmental comfort, passenger briefing/procedures, fuel planning (normal, long-range, over water). Discuss anti-icing system, airframe icing hazards.

Flight: Pilot not flying duties (normal procedures, normal checklists, simulated emergency procedures and abnormal checklists); Pilot Flying (approaches and landings).

Performance Standard. Demonstrate safe and proficient air work and effective cockpit management. Operate the aircraft according to the NFM, IFM and FARs. Demonstrate sound Crew Resource Management (CRM).

Prerequisite. 2101

CP-2401   2.0   365   B,R   (N*)   A   1 UC-12W

Goal. Review right seat (pilot not flying) navigation, communication, and cockpit management duties. Review right seat approaches and landings.

Requirements

Brief: Aircraft servicing, NATOPS - Chapter 29 Flight Crew Coordination, ditching, weather radar, satellite phone, cabin ICS and audio capabilities, passenger/environmental comfort, passenger briefing/procedures, fuel planning (normal, long-range, over water). Discuss TAWS system, windshear hazards, windshear recognition and windshear avoidance/escape maneuvers.

Flight: Review pilot not flying duties (normal procedures, normal checklists, simulated emergency procedures and abnormal checklists); Pilot Flying (approaches and landings).

Performance Standard. Demonstrate safe and proficient air work and effective cockpit management. Operate the aircraft according to the NFM, IFM and FARs. Demonstrate sound Crew Resource Management (CRM).

Prerequisite. 2101, 2400

6. Familiarization Review (FAM REV)

   a. Purpose. Review UC-12W FAM procedures.

   b. General. Basic Pilots shall be trained and evaluated in the left seat.

   c. Crew Requirements. PUI shall be instructed/evaluated by an NI/ANI.

FAM REV-2500 2.0 * B D A 1 UC-12W

Goal. Complete FAM Review.

Requirement. Conduct an objective review of the Pilot's knowledge of mission planning, normal operating procedures (flight and ground), crew resource management, aircraft systems, performance criteria, emergency procedures, and debriefing. The focus is on normal and emergency procedures. Emphasis shall be placed on the aforementioned items with the addition of local course rules, unit SOP, and admin flight procedures. This review is the means to measure the Pilot's efficiency in the execution of normal operating procedures and reaction to emergencies and malfunctions. Review all previous requirements in preparation for upgrade/designation.

Performance Standard. Demonstrate satisfactory knowledge of aircraft operating procedures and limitations. Demonstrate safe and proficient air work and show the ability to recognize deviation from Airline Transport Pilot (ATP) Practical Test Standards (PTS) standards and work towards correction. Operate the aircraft according to the NFM, IFM and FARs.

Prerequisite. 2101, 2200, 2201, 2300, 2401

209. MISSION SKILL (3000 PHASE)

1. General. All Mission Skill events shall be instructed by an NI or ANI.

2. Operational Support Airlift

OSA-3100 2.0 60 B,R (N*) A 1 UC-12W

Goal. Conduct an Operational Support Airlift (OSA) mission.

Requirements

Brief: Mission and crew coordination, flight planning, weather, fuel requirements, weight and balance, aircraft performance factors, RON, passenger requirements, Scheduling Agency (JOSAC/MCB Japan) coordination, and emergency procedures. Demonstrate use of cargo door. Discuss rapid decompression, door open annunciation emergency procedures in flight.

Flight: Conduct an OSA mission.

Performance Standard. Demonstrate satisfactory knowledge of aircraft systems, operating procedures and limitations. Demonstrate safe and proficient air work and show the ability to recognize deviation from Airline Transport Pilot (ATP) Practical Test Standards (PTS) standards and work towards correction. Operate the aircraft according to the NFM, IFM and FARs.

Prerequisite. 2000 Phase complete, 6100, 6101.

3. Air Logistics Support

ALS-3200   2.0   60   B,R   (N*)   A   1 UC-12W

Goal. Conduct an Air Logistics Support (ALS) mission.

Requirements

Brief: Mission and crew coordination, flight planning, weather, fuel requirements, weight and balance, aircraft performance factors, RON, scheduling agency (JOSAC, MCB-Japan) coordination, cargo certification and handling, special cargo considerations, and emergency procedures.

Flight: Conduct an ALS mission.

Performance Standard. Demonstrate satisfactory knowledge of aircraft operating procedures and limitations. Demonstrate safe and proficient air work and show the ability to recognize deviation from Airline Transport Pilot (ATP) Practical Test Standards (PTS) standards and work towards correction. Operate the aircraft according to the NFM, IFM and FARs.

Prerequisite. 2000 Phase complete, 6100, 6101.

210. CORE PLUS (4000 PHASE)

1. General

a. The Core Plus Phase consists of academic, skill, and mission training.

b. Core Plus training is defined as theater specific and/or low likelihood of occurrence training and should not be the focus of unit training.

c. The Pilot should be Core Skill complete prior to beginning the Core Plus Phase of training.

d. Shall be instructed/evaluated by an NI/ANI.

2. Core Plus Academics (ACAD)

ACAD-4000   2.0   *   B,R   CLRM   ASE Academics

General. At the publishing date of this manual, the ASE academic period of instruction is under development by the Syllabus Sponsor (VMR Det Belle Chase) and it will be distributed to the UC-12W community once completed.

ACAD-4001   4.0   730   B,R   CLRM   International

Goal. Pilot under instruction is introduced to mission planning for extended over water and overseas operations.

Requirements. The PUI will be introduced to mission planning for a multiday, long range flight that should include the crossing of international airspace. The following tools commonly used for mission planning in the international environment should be introduced: Optimum Path Aircraft Routing System (OPARS), Aircraft/Personnel Automated Clearance System (APACS), Foreign Clearance Guide, Area Planning/General Planning (AP/GP), Giant Report/Global Decision Support System 2 (GDSS2) account, Naval Flight Information Group (NavFIG), Jeppesen View and the validation and use of Jeppesen terminal approach procedures, Universal Flight Planning software for oceanic remote operations, North Atlantic/Pacific Tracks message, North Atlantic/Pacific Track Oceanic Checklist, North Atlantic/Pacific Minimum Navigation Performance Specification Airspace Operations Manual, Equal Time Point (ETP)/Point of No Return (PNR), and Aircraft Flight Manual (AFM) Supplement 63. The following contingency and emergency operations will also be discussed: engine failure (drift down), loss of pressurization, lost communication, and weather avoidance/contingency operations in an RVSM and/or non radar environment. Discuss ditching, post ditching aircraft evacuation procedures.

Performance Standard. Successful completion of the course of instruction.

ACAD-4002   2.0   730   B,R   CLRM MIL International

General. At the publishing date of this manual, the MIL International academic period of instruction is under development by the Syllabus Sponsor (VMR Det Belle Chase) and it will be distributed to the UC-12W community once completed.

3. Assault Support (AS)

   a. General

      Procedures are designed to remain within the capabilities envelope of the aircraft and to maximize the protection capabilities of the ASE in the take-off and landing environment.

      Note: Detailed procedures for this event are being developed by the syllabus sponsor (VMR JRB Belle Chase, LA). Once the maneuvers have been approved they will be released to the units.

b. Purpose

Develop skills for operations that take place in a Low Threat
(Permissive) environment and will include specific procedures to
minimize aircraft exposure to a threat.

Upon completion of this stage, the pilot will be capable of
flying in a ground threat environment during day or night.

Develop proficiency in the use of Electronic Warfare Principles,
Aircraft Survivability Equipment (ASE), and threat reactions
versus enemy surface-to-air threats.

AS-4100   2.0   730   B,R   D   A   1 UC-12W

General. At the publishing date of this manual, the Assault
Support/ASE flight is under development by the Syllabus Sponsor
(VMR Det Belle Chase) and it will be distributed to the UC-12W
community once completed.

Prerequisite. 4000

4. Expeditionary Shore-Based Operations (EXP). Expeditionary operations are
defined as operations to certified unimproved runways to include dirt, grass
or gravel only.

EXP-4200   2.0   730   B,R   (N*)   A   1 UC-12W

Goal. Conduct operations to certified unimproved runways to
include dirt and grass.

Requirements. Conduct aviation operations to certified
unimproved runways in accordance with the limitations and
guidelines in the NATOPS manual.

Brief: The brief should include considerations for the
specific type of runway to be used, including but not limited to:
surface effects on runway length (takeoff, aborted takeoff,
landing, etc). The following contingency and emergency operations
will also be discussed: engine failure on take-off (before &
after V1), single engine landing (specifically use of single
engine reverse thrust), and abnormal flap configurations for
landing. ANI/NI shall discuss high altitude airfield planning
factors and aircraft high density altitude performance decrements
for operations from airports or temporary landing zones
constructed at 8,000 feet mean sea level.

Conduct: PUI to conduct landings and takeoffs from certified
unimproved runways (dirt or grass). PUI shall conduct all take-
offs and landings from the left seat. A minimum of three normal
T/O and landings to a full stop (no simulated emergency/abnormal
conditions) are required for sortie completion.

Performance Standard. Demonstrate safe landing and takeoff
procedures from one of the two categories of certified unimproved
runway surfaces. Operate the aircraft according to the NFM, IFM,
FARs and ICAO procedures.

Prerequisite. 2000 Phase complete, 6100, 6101.

5. International Procedures (INT)

INT-4300   3.0   730   B,R   (N*)   A   1 UC-12W

> Goal. Pilot under instruction performs extended range operations and alternates between left and right seats throughout the mission in order to demonstrate flight leadership from either seat.
>
> Requirement. PUI shall demonstrate the ability to supervise preflight preparation and manage a crew and aircraft away from home station on an operational mission that should include a RON.
>
> Brief: Mission coordination, flight planning, weather, fuel planning, load computations, performance, CRM.
>
> Conduct: PUI shall demonstrate flight leadership and Crew Resource Management by acting as the TAC during an operational mission that includes a RON. During the trip, the PUI shall conduct a two-engine instrument approach.
>
> Performance Standard. Operate the aircraft according to the NFM IFM, FARs and ICAO procedures.
>
> Prerequisite. 4001

INT-4301   3.0   730   B,R   (N*)   A   1 UC-12W

> Goal. Pilot Under Instruction conducts overwater navigation. Evaluation leg should be conducted with the PUI in the left or right seat.
>
> Requirement. PUI to demonstrate the ability to manage a crew and aircraft on an extended, overwater flight under ICAO rules.
>
> Brief: Mission coordination, crew briefing, ATFP briefing coordination, flight planning, weather brief, fuel planning, weight and balance, aircraft inspection, cargo inspection (as required), manifest inspection, trip aircraft clearance, foreign clearance guide review, survival gear inspection, fuel computations, performance, customs, and agriculture inspection.
>
> Conduct: PUI to conduct overwater navigation in accordance with ICAO, FAR and NATOPS convention. The following contingency and emergency operations will also be discussed: engine failure (drift down), loss of pressurization, lost communication, and weather avoidance/contingency operations in an RVSM and or non radar environment. During the trip, the PUI shall conduct a two-engine instrument approach and landing from the left seat.
>
> Performance Standard. Operate the aircraft according to the NFM IFM, FARs and ICAO procedures.
>
> Prerequisite. 4001

211. INSTRUCTOR TRAINING (5000 PHASE)

1. General. The Instructor Phase consists of four events leading to NATOPS Instructor and Assistant NATOPS Designations.

2. Instructor Under Training (IUT)

IUT-5100   2.0   *   B,R   D   E   A   1 UC-12W

Goal. NI/ANI Training

Requirements

Introduce the IUT to the skills required to correct common
student errors and prepare the IUT to conduct T&R syllabus and
NATOPS/Instrument evaluation flights IAW Chap. 30 of the NATOPS
Manual and OPNAV 3710.7.

    Brief: Training Areas, Maneuver Descriptions, Operating
Limitations, EP/Abnormals, Aeromedical Factors, Aerodynamics

    Flight: Flight Planning, Weight & Balance, Performance
Planning, Flight/Mission Briefing, Preflight/Postflight, Start,
Taxi & Takeoff, Steep Turns, Slow Flight, Stalls, Fuel
Management, Emergency Descent, Holding, Precision Approach, Wave
Off(s), Non-Precision Approaches, Single Engine Work, Reduced
Flap Landings, Contract Maintenance Procedures

Performance Standard. The IUT shall be evaluated on the ability
to correctly brief the flight, demonstrate and introduce
maneuvers in accordance with applicable directives, correct
student deficiencies, conduct proper debrief and display
appropriate subject matter expertise.

External Syllabus Support. Approved working area or restricted
area.

Prerequisite. 6402, Standardization Board recommendation

IUT-5101   2.0   *   B,R   D   E   A   1 UC-12W

Goal. NI/ANI Training

Requirements

Introduce the IUT to the skills required to correct common
student errors and prepare the IUT to conduct T&R syllabus and
NATOPS/Instrument evaluation flights from the right seat IAW
Chap. 30 of the NATOPS Manual and OPNAV 3710.7.

    Brief: Operating Limitations, EP/Abnormals, Aeromedical
Factors, Aerodynamics

    Flight: Flight Planning, Weight & Balance, Performance
Planning, Flight/Mission Briefing, Preflight/Postflight, Start,
Taxi & Takeoff, Steep Turns, Slow Flight, Stalls, Fuel
Management, Emergency Descent, Holding, Precision Approach, Wave
Off(s), Non-Precision Approaches, Single Engine Work, Reduced
Flap Landings, Contract Maintenance Procedures

Performance Standard. The IUT shall be evaluated on the ability
to correctly brief the flight, demonstrate and introduce
maneuvers in accordance with applicable directives, correct
student deficiencies, conduct proper debrief and display
appropriate subject matter expertise.

External Syllabus Support. Approved working area or restricted
area.

Prerequisite. 5100

IUT-5102   2.0   *   B,R   D   E   A   1 UC-12W

Goal. NI/ANI Training

Requirements

IUT shall refine the skills required to correct common student errors and prepare to conduct T&R syllabus and NATOPS/Instrument evaluation flights IAW Chap. 30 of the NATOPS Manual and OPNAV 3710.7.

    Brief: Operating Limitations, EP/Abnormals, Aeromedical Factors, Aerodynamics

    Flight: Flight Planning, Weight & Balance, Performance Planning, Flight/Mission Briefing, Preflight/Postflight, Start, Taxi & Takeoff, Steep Turns, Slow Flight, Stalls, Fuel Management, Emergency Descent, Holding, Precision Approach, Wave Off(s), Non-Precision Approaches, Single Engine Work, Reduced Flap Landings, Contract Maintenance Procedures

Performance Standard. The IUT shall be evaluated on the ability to correctly brief the flight, demonstrate and introduce maneuvers in accordance with applicable directives, correct student deficiencies, conduct proper debrief and display appropriate subject matter expertise.

External Syllabus Support. Approved working area or restricted area.

Prerequisite. 5101

IUT-5103   2.0   *   B,R   D   E   A   1 UC-12W

Goal. NI/ANI Check

Requirements

IUT shall be evaluated on the skills required to correct common student errors and conduct T&R syllabus and NATOPS/Instrument evaluation flights from the right seat IAW Chap. 30 of the NATOPS Manual and OPNAV 3710.7. Flight should be completed in conjunction with a NATOPS/Instrument evaluation.

    Brief: Operating Limitations, EP/Abnormals, Aeromedical Factors, Aerodynamics

    Flight: Flight Planning, Weight & Balance, Performance Planning, Flight/Mission Briefing, Preflight/Postflight, Start, Taxi & Takeoff, Steep Turns, Slow Flight, Stalls, Fuel Management, Emergency Descent, Holding, Precision Approach, Wave Off(s), Non-Precision Approaches, Single Engine Work, Reduced Flap Landings, Contract Maintenance Procedures

Performance Standard. The IUT shall be evaluated on the ability to correctly brief the flight, demonstrate and introduce maneuvers in accordance with applicable directives, correct student deficiencies, conduct proper debrief and display appropriate subject matter expertise.

External Syllabus Support. Approved working area or restricted area.

Prerequisite. 5102

212. REQUIREMENTS, QUALIFICATIONS, DESIGNATIONS (RQD) (6000 PHASE)

1. UC-12W RQD Academics

ACAD-6000   4.0   365   B,R   E   NATOPS Open Book

    Goal. The open book examination shall consist of, but not be limited to the question bank. The purpose of the open book examination is to evaluate the Pilot's knowledge of the appropriate publications and the aircraft.

    Performance Standard. Achieve a minimum score of 3.5 on the open book examination.

ACAD-6001   2.0   365   B,R   E   NATOPS Closed Book

    Goal. The purpose of the closed book examination is to evaluate the Pilot's knowledge of normal/emergency procedures and aircraft limitations.

    Performance Standard. Achieve a minimum score of 3.3 on the closed book examination.

    Prerequisite. 6000

ACAD-6002   2.0   365   B,R   E   NATOPS Oral

    Goal. The oral examination shall consist of, but not be limited to the question bank. The instructor may draw upon their experience to ask questions of a direct and objective nature to evaluate the Pilot's knowledge of normal/emergency procedures, aircraft limitations, and performance.

    Performance Standard. Achieve a minimum grade of qualified on the oral examination.

    Prerequisite. 6000,6001

ACAD-6003   8.0   365   B,R   E   Instrument Ground School

    Goal. The Instrument Ground School shall be an approved Commander Naval Air Forces (CNAF) syllabus. If an approved Instrument Ground School is not available this requirement may be waived.

    Performance Standard. Achieve a minimum grade of qualified for Instrument Ground School.

ACAD-6004   2.0   365   B,R   E   Instrument Exam

    Goal. Successful completion of the Instrument Examination.

    Performance Standard. Achieve a minimum passing score on the Instrument Examination.

    Prerequisite. 6003

ACAD-6005   2.0   365   B,R   E   Instrument Oral Exam

    Goal. The oral NATOPS instrument examination shall consist of, but not be limited to the question bank in addition to any subject listed for coverage in OPNAVINST 3710.7.

    Performance Standard. Achieve a minimum grade of qualified on the oral NATOPS instrument examination.

    Prerequisite. 6004

ACAD-6006   1.0   365   B,R   E   CRM BASIC

Goal. Introduce multi-piloted Crew Resource Management.

Requirement. This course of instruction is included in initial and Recurrent CACT.

ACAD-6007   1.0   365   B,R   E   CRM UC-12W

Goal. This course of instruction is under development by VMR Det Belle Chase, LA and will be distributed to the UC-12W community once completed.

ACAD-6008   2.0   365   B,R   E   FCP Open Book Examination

Goal. The open book examination shall consist of 20 to 30 questions, including, but not limited to information from Chapter 10 of NATOPS 1A-C12WA-NFM-000. The purpose of the open book examination is to evaluate the Pilot's knowledge of FCF procedures and the aircraft systems and limitations.

Performance Standard. Achieve a minimum score of 3.5 on the open book examination.

ACAD-6009   1.0   30   B,R   E   Monthly EP Examination

Goal. Successfully complete the UC-12W Monthly Emergency Procedures Examination.

Requirement. Pass the Monthly Emergency Procedures Examination.

Performance Standard. Achieve a passing score on the Monthly Emergency Procedures Examination.

2. NATOPS Evaluation

NTPS-6100   2.0   365   B,R   (N*)   E   A/S   1 UC-12W/SIM

Goal. Complete annual NATOPS flight evaluation. Conduct an objective evaluation of the Pilot's knowledge of mission planning, normal operating procedures (flight and ground), crew resource management, aircraft systems, performance criteria, emergency procedures, and debriefing. The focus is on normal and emergency procedures. Emphasis shall be placed on the aforementioned items with the addition of local course rules, unit SOP, and admin flight procedures. The NATOPS evaluation is intended to evaluate compliance with NATOPS procedures. The NATOPS evaluation is the means to measure the Pilot's efficiency in the execution of normal operating procedures and reaction to emergencies and malfunctions. The NATOPS evaluation process should be as much a learning tool and/or experience as it is an evaluation.

Requirement. Demonstrate comprehensive knowledge and understanding of NATOPS, unit SOP, and local course rules.

Performance Standard. Executes flight and ground operations safely IAW OPNAV 3710.7, NATOPS and applicable manuals. Complies with unit SOP and local course rules.

Prerequisite. Core Skill Phase complete, ACPM 83XX Phase complete; 6000, 6001, 6002.

NTPS-6103   0.0   90   B,R   (N⁺)   E   A   1 UC-12W (static)

    Goal. Quarterly NATOPS static aircraft emergency procedures review.

    Requirement. This review should cover selected aircraft emergencies in a static aircraft. This event can be completed in conjunction with a flight. Demonstrate comprehensive knowledge and understanding of NATOPS emergencies.

    Performance Standard. Executes the review in accordance with NATOPS.

3. Instrument Evaluations

INST-6101   2.0   365   B,R   (N⁺)   E   A/S   1 UC-12W/SIM

    Goal. Complete standard instrument flight evaluation. Following completion of the ground evaluation events, a standard instrument flight evaluation event shall be flown and completed with a grade of "Qualified." Conduct an objective evaluation of the airman's knowledge of flight planning, filing, briefing, conduct of flight under normal operating conditions, emergency procedures, closing out flight plans, and debriefing.

    Requirement. Demonstrate comprehensive knowledge and understanding of instrument flight procedures, NATOPS, unit SOP, and local course rules.

    Performance Standard. Executes flight and ground operations safely IAW OPNAV 3710.7, NATOPS, NATOPS Instrument Flight Manual, and training rules.

    Prerequisite. 2500,6004,6005

INST-6102   2.0   365   B,R   (N⁺)   E   A/S   1 UC-12W/SIM

    Goal. Complete special instrument flight evaluation. Following completion of the ground evaluation events, a special instrument flight evaluation event shall be flown and completed with a grade of "Qualified." Conduct an objective evaluation of the airman's knowledge of flight planning, filing, briefing, conduct of flight under normal operating conditions, emergency procedures, closing out flight plans, and debriefing.

    Requirement. Demonstrate comprehensive knowledge and understanding of instrument flight procedures, NATOPS, unit SOP, and local course rules.

    Performance Standard. Executes flight and ground operations safely IAW OPNAV 3710.7, NATOPS, NATOPS Instrument Flight Manual, and training rules.

    Prerequisite. Meets OPNAVINST 3710.7 Special Instrument requirements, recommended by Stan Board, 2500, 6004, 6005

4. Transport 2 Pilot (T2P)

T2P-6300   1.5   365   B,R   D   E   A   1 UC-12W

    Goal. T2P evaluation flight.

Requirement. Demonstrate a thorough knowledge of the aircraft systems, the ability to perform the responsibilities of a Second-in-Command (SIC)/copilot, and the ability to assist the TPC in all aircraft configurations under varying emergency and meteorological conditions.

> Brief: Flight planning, weight and balance, fuel computations, knowledge and use of the Flight Management System (FMS) and normal and emergency procedures.

> Flight: Demonstrate a proficiency in the use of all checklists, taxi & run-up procedures, normal/crosswind Take-offs and landings, aircraft handling (high work), use of the FMS in enroute & terminal operations, airstarts, emergency descent, instrument approach procedures, circle to land, missed approach procedures, single engine operations and after landing and post flight procedures.

Performance Standard. NFM.

Prerequisite. 2000 PHASE COMPLETE, 6000, 6001, 6300, 6101, 6103

5. Transport Aircraft Commander (TAC)

TAC-6400   1.5   *   B   (N*)   E   A   1 UC-12W

Goal. TAC Mission Procedures Review.

Requirements. Conduct a simulated airlift mission to demonstrate a thorough knowledge of NATOPS, scheduling agency (JOSAC/MCBJapan) Unit procedures and FAR's in a real world environment. Demonstrate a thorough knowledge of Crew Resource Management (CRM) and Operational Risk Management (ORM). Demonstrate the ability to perform the responsibilities of a Pilot-in-Command during normal operations in high volume/density airspace.

> Brief: Flight planning, weight and balance, fuel computations and management, knowledge and use of the Flight Management System (FMS) and scheduling agency (JOSAC/MCB Japan) procedures and requirements.

> Flight: Demonstrate a proficiency in the use of all checklists, normal procedures, use of the FMS in enroute & terminal operations to include RNAV SIDS & STARS, instrument approach procedures and post flight procedures.

Performance Standard. NFM, FAR

Prerequisite. 3000 Phase Complete, 6300

TAC-6401   1.5   *   B   D   E   A   1 UC-12W

Goal. TPC Pre-Check flight.

Requirement. Demonstrate a thorough knowledge of the aircraft systems, normal and emergency procedures, FAR's and JOSAC procedures. Demonstrate a thorough knowledge of Crew Resource Management (CRM) and Operational Risk Management (ORM). Demonstrate the ability to perform the responsibilities of a Pilot-in-Command in all aircraft configurations and under varying emergency and meteorological conditions.

Brief: Flight planning, weight and balance, fuel computations, knowledge and use of the Flight Management System (FMS) and normal and emergency procedures.

Flight: Demonstrate a proficiency in the use of all checklists, taxi & run-up procedures, normal/crosswind Take-offs and landings, aircraft handling (high work), use of the FMS in en route & terminal operations, air starts, emergency descent, instrument approach procedures, circle to land, missed approach procedures, single engine operations and after landing and post flight procedures.

Performance Standard. NFM

Prerequisite. 6400

TAC-6402   2.0   365   B,R   D   E   A   1 UC-12W

Goal. TPC Check flight.

Requirement. Demonstrate a thorough knowledge of the aircraft systems, normal and emergency procedures, FAR's and scheduling agency (JOSAC/MCB Japan) procedures. Demonstrate a thorough knowledge of Crew Resource Management (CRM) and Operational Risk Management (ORM). Demonstrate the ability to perform the responsibilities of a Pilot-in-Command in all aircraft configurations and under varying emergency and meteorological conditions.

Brief: Flight planning, weight and balance, fuel computations, knowledge and use of the Flight Management System (FMS) and normal and emergency procedures.

Flight: Demonstrate a proficiency in the use of all checklists, taxi & run-up procedures, normal/crosswind Take-offs and landings, aircraft handling (high work), use of the FMS in enroute & terminal operations, airstarts, emergency descent, instrument approach procedures, circle to land, missed approach procedures, single engine operations and after landing and post flight procedures.

Performance Standard. NFM

Prerequisite. 3000 Phase complete, 6000, 6001, 6002, 6401

7. Functional Check Pilot (FCP)

FCP-6500   3.5   *   B   D   E   A   1 UC-12W

Goal. Instruct an NI/ANI on the safe and proper conduct of an FCF. This does not necessarily entail conducting an entire "A" profile in flight.

Requirements. The flight shall consist of execution and/or discussion of all "A" profile functional check flight procedures from the left seat and be instructed by a qualified FCP Pilot.

Brief: FCP Responsibilities, Briefing, Check Fight Profiles, Crew Coordination, Aircraft Limitations, Preflight, Start Procedures, Checklists, Stall/Spin Recovery, Airstart Procedures, Operating Limitations; Engine Performance, Pressurization, Bleed Air System, Aerodynamic, Avionic/Flight

Instrument, Hydraulic System, and Electrical System Checks; Approach and Recovery, and Landing

Flight: Preflight, Start Procedures, Checklists, Approach to Stalls, Airstart Procedures, Operating Limitations; Engine Performance, Pressurization, Bleed Air System, Aerodynamic, Avionic/Flight Instrument, Hydraulic System, and Electrical System Checks; Approach and Recovery, and Landing

Performance Standard. Satisfactorily execute procedures per the NFM and IAW OPNAVINST 3710.7_.

External Syllabus Support. Approved working area or restricted area.

Prerequisite. 5103,6008,6402,Standardization Board recommendation

FCP-6501   3.5   *   B,R   D   E   A   1 UC-12W

Goal. FCP Evaluation/Designation

Requirements. The flight shall consist of execution and/or discussion of all "A" profile functional check flight procedures from the right seat and be evaluated by a qualified FCP Pilot.

Brief: FCP Responsibilities, Briefing, Check Fight Profiles, Crew Coordination, Aircraft Limitations, Preflight, Start Procedures, Checklists, Stall/Spin Recovery, Airstart Procedures, Operating Limitations; Engine Performance, Pressurization, Bleed Air System, Aerodynamic, Avionic/Flight Instrument, Hydraulic System, and Electrical System Checks; Approach and Recovery, and Landing

Flight: Preflight, Start Procedures, Checklists, Approach to Stalls, Airstart Procedures, Operating Limitations; Engine Performance, Pressurization, Bleed Air System, Aerodynamic, Avionic/Flight Instrument, Hydraulic System, and Electrical System Checks; Approach and Recovery, and Landing

Performance Standard. Satisfactorily execute procedures per the NFM and IAW OPNAVINST 3710.7_.

External Syllabus Support. Approved working area or restricted area.

Prerequisite. 6500

213. AVIATION CAREER PROGRESSION MODEL (8000 PHASE)

1. Purpose

a. To enhance professional understanding of Marine Aviation and the MAGTF and ensure individuals possess the requisite skills to fill battle command and battle staff positions in support of the ACE and the MAGTF in a joint environment. The focus of training in the Aviation Career Progression Model (ACPM) is on academic events in the following areas:

Marine Air Command and Control System (MACCS)

Aviation Ground Support

Joint Air Operations

ACE Battle Staff

MAGTF

Seabased Operations
Combatant Commander Organizations

b. All tactical T/M/S T&R manuals have ACPM training requirements embedded within the progressive training phases, including the flight leadership POI. If not already completed prior to assignment to VMR-1 or a VMR det (C-9, UC-35, C-12, or C-20), pilots assigned to an OSA platform shall complete ACPM training requirements as outlined per their original T/M/S MOS T&R manual. Refer to NAVMC 3500.14, Aviation T&R Program Manual, as a primary reference for ACPM training requirements.

2. General

a. The ACPM is intended to be an integrated series of academic events contained within each phase of training. Accordingly, ACPM academic events are like any other academic event in that they serve as pre-requisites to selected flight events or stages. Additionally, several ACPM academic events are integrated as prerequisites for flight leadership syllabi.

b. ACPM academic events, along with their identifying prerequisite association with other training phases/stages/events are listed below.

	VMR-1 VMR Det (UC-12W)			
	ACPM TO UC-12W T&R MATRIX			
STAGE	EVENT NUMBER	CLASS	ACPM DESCRIPTION	PREREQUISITE TO (PHASE/STAGE/EVENT)
ACPM	8200	(U)	MACCS AGENCIES, FUNCTIONS AND CONTROL OF AIRCRAFT AND MISSLES	2000 PHASE
ACPM	8201	(U)	MWCS BRIEF	2000 PHASE
ACPM	8202	(U)	ACA AND AIRSPACE	2000 PHASE
ACPM	8210	(U)	AVIATION GROUND SUPPORT	2000 PHASE
ACPM	8230	(U)	ACE BATTLESTAFF	2000 PHASE
ACPM	8231	(U)	BATTLE COMMAND DISPLAY	2000 PHASE
ACPM	8240	(U)	SIX FUNCTIONS OF MARINE AVIATION	2000 PHASE
ACPM	8241	(U)	JTAR/ASR INTRODUCTION AND PRACTICAL APPLICATION CLASS	2000 PHASE
ACPM	8242	(U)	SITE COMMAND PRIMER	2000 PHASE
ACPM	8250	(U)	THEATER AIR GROUND SYSTEM (TAGS)	2000 PHASE
ACPM	8300	(U)	AIR DEFENSE	3000 PHASE
ACPM	8310	(U)	FORWARD ARMING AND REFUELING POINT (FARP) OPERATIONS	3000 PHASE
ACPM	8311	(U)	MARINE CORPS TACTICAL FUEL SYSTEMS	3000 PHASE
ACPM	8320	(U)	JOINT STRUCTURE & JOINT AIR OPERATIONS	3000 PHASE
ACPM	8321	(U)	JOINT AIR TASKING CYCLE PHASE 1: STRATEGY DEVELOPMENT	3000 PHASE
ACPM	8322	(U)	JOINT AIR TASKING CYCLE PHASE 2: TARGET DEVELOPMENT	3000 PHASE
ACPM	8323	(U)	JOINT AIR TASKING CYCLE PHASE 3: WEAPONING AND ALLOCATION	3000 PHASE
ACPM	8324	(U)	JOINT AIR TASKING CYCLE PHASE 4: JOINT ATO PRODUCTION	3000 PHASE
ACPM	8325	(U)	JOINT AIR TASKING CYCLE PHASE 5:	3000 PHASE
ACPM	8326	(U)	JOINT AIR TASKING CYCLE PHASE 6: COMBAT ASSESMENT	3000 PHASE
ACPM	8340	(U)	INTEGRATING FIRES AND AIRSPACE WITHIN THE MAGTF	3000 PHASE
ACPM	8350	(U)	PHASING CONTROL ASHORE	3000 PHASE
ACPM	8351	(U)	TACRON ORGANIZATIONS AND FUNCTIONS	3000 PHASE
ACPM	8630	(U)	TACTICAL AIR COMMAND CENTER (TACC)	6000 PHASE
ACPM	8660	(U)	JOINT OPS INTRO	6000 PHASE
ACPM	8640	(U)	JOINT DATA NETWORK	6000 PHASE
ACPM	8641	(U)	MAGTF THEATER	6000 PHASE
ACPM	8620	(U)	ESG/CSG INTEGRATION	6000 PHASE

214. UC-12W T&R SYLLABUS MATRIX

UC-12W PILOT T&R MATRIX

STAGE	TRNG CODE	T&R DESCRIPTION	POI	DEVICE E	# OF A/C	CON	RE FLY	# OF ACAD	ACAD TIME	# OF SIM	SIM TIME	# OF FLTS	FLT TIME	PREREQUISITE	NOTES	CHAINING	EVENT CONV
		CORE SKILL-INTRODUCTION TRAINING (1000 PHASE EVENTS)															
		CORE SKILL ACADEMICS															
ACAD	1000	CACT GND SCHL INITIAL	B				*		48.0								
ACAD	1001	CACT GND SCHL REFRESH	B				365		8.0					1000			
ACAD	1002	RVSM	B				*		3.0								
ACAD	1003	WEATHER RADAR	B,R				365		2.0								
ACAD	1004	CACT INTERNATIONAL PROCEDURES INITIAL	B,R				*		21.0								
ACAD	1005	CACT INTERNATIONAL PROCEDURES RECURRENT	R				730		8.0					1004			
		ACAD TOTAL						6	90.0	0	0.0	0	0.0				
		COMMAND AIRCRAFT CREW TRAINING (CACT)															
CACT	1101	CACT SIM 1	B	S		(N*)	*				4.0						
CACT	1102	CACT SIM 2	B	S		(N*)	*				4.0						
CACT	1103	CACT SIM 3	B	S		(N*)	*				4.0						
CACT	1104	CACT SIM 4	B	S		(N*)	*				4.0						
CACT	1105	CACT SIM 5	B,R	S		(N*)	365				4.0						
CACT	1106	CACT SIM 6	B,R	S		(N*)	365				4.0						
CACT	1107	CACT SIM 7	B,R	S		(N*)	365				4.0						
		CACT INT SIM TOTAL						0	0.0	7	28.0	0	0.0				
		CORE SKILL INTRODUCTION TRAINING (1000 PHASE EVENTS) TOTAL						6	90.0	7	28.0	0	0.0				
		CORE SKILL TRAINING (2000 PHASE)															
		CORE SKILL ACADEMICS (ACAD)															
ACAD	2000	INTRO LOCAL PROC	B,R			D	*		3.0					1000, 1001, CACT COMP, 1107			
ACAD	2001	FMS PROCEDURES	B,R			D	*		3.0					2000			
		TOTAL ACAD STAGE						2	6.0	0	0.0	0	0.0				
		FAMILIARIZATION (FAM)															
FAM	2100	INTRO UC-12W A/C	B	A	1	D	*						2.0	2000,2001			
FAM	2101	INTRO EXPANDED ENVELOPE	B,R	A	1	D	365						2.0	2100			
		TOTAL FAM STAGE						0	0.0	0	0.0	2	4.0				

UC-12W PILOT T&R MATRIX

STAGE	TRNG CODE	T&R DESCRIPTION	POI	DEVICE E	# OF A/C	CON	RE FLY	# OF ACAD	ACAD TIME	# OF SIM	SIM TIME	# OF FLTS	FLT TIME	PREREQUISITE	NOTES	CHAINING	EVENT CONV
		INSTRUMENTS (INST)															
INST	2200	INTRO INST NAV	B,R	A	1	(N*)	*						2.0	2101			
INST	2201	HIGH ALT OPS	B,R	A	1	(N*)	365					2	2.0	2101			
		TOTAL INST STAGE						0	0.0	0	0.0	2	4.0				
		NIGHT FAMILIARIZATION (NFAM)															
NFAM	2300	INTRO NIGHT OPS	B,R	A	1	N*	180					1	1.5	2101			
		TOTAL NFAM STAGE						0	0.0	0	0.0	1	1.5				
		CO-PILOT RESPONSIBILITIES (CP)															
CP	2400	INTRO CP RESP	B	A	1	(N*)	*						2.0	2101	RS		
CP	2401	PRACTICE CP RESP	B,R	A	1	(N*)	365					2	2.0	2400,2101	RS		
		TOTAL CP STAGE						0	0.0	0	0.0	2	4.0				
		FAMILIARIZATION REVIEW (FAM REV)															
FAM REV	2500	PRAC FAM MANEUVERS	B	A	1	D	*					1	2.0	2101,2201,2200,2300,240		2101,2401,2300~N	
		TOTAL REV STAGE						0	0.0	0	0.0	1	2.0				
		CORE SKILL TRAINING (2000 PHASE EVENTS) TOTAL						2	6.0	0	0.0	8	15.5				
		MISSION SKILL TRAINING (3000 PHASE)															
		OPERATIONAL SUPPORT AIRLIFT (OSA)															
OSA	3100	OSA	B,R	A	1	(N*)	60						2.0	2000 PHASE COMPLETE, 6100,6101	PAX	2201,2401,3200,2300~N	
		TOTAL OSA STAGE						0	0.0	0	0.0	1	2.0				
		AIR LOGISTICS SUPPORT (ALS)															
ALS	3200	ALS	B,R	A	1	(N*)	60						2.0	2000 PHASE COMPLETE, 6100,6101	CARGO	2201,2401,3100,2300~N	
		TOTAL ALS STAGE						0	0.0	0	0.0	1	2.0				
		TOTAL MISSION SKILL TRAINING (3000 PHASE EVENTS)						0	0.0	0	0.0	2	4.0				

UC-12W PILOT T&R MATRIX

STAGE	TRNG CODE	T&R DESCRIPTION	POI	DEVICE E	DEVICE A/C	# OF A/C	CON	RE FLY	# OF ACAD	ACAD TIME	# OF SIM	SIM TIME	# OF FLTS	FLT TIME	PREREQUISITE	NOTES	CHAINING	EVENT CONV
		CORE PLUS TRAINING (4000 PHASE)																
		CORE PLUS ACADEMICS																
ACAD	4000	ASE Academics	B,R					*		2.0								
ACAD	4001	CACT International Procedures	B,R					730		4.0								
ACAD	4002	Military International Procedures	B,R					730		2.0					1002			
		TOTAL ACAD STAGE							3	8.0	0		0					
		ASSAULT SUPPORT (AS)																
AS	4100	ASE Procedures	B,R		A	1	D	730	0	0.0	0	0.0	1	2.0	4000	ASE	3100,3200	
		TOTAL AS STAGE							0	0.0	0	0.0	1	2.0				
		EXPEDITIONARY SHORE-BASED OPERATIONS (EXP)																
EXP	4200	Unimproved Runway Operations	B,R		A	1	(N*)	*	0	0.0	0	0.0	1	2.0	2000 PHASE Complete, 6100, 6101		3100,3200	
		TOTAL EXP STAGE							0	0.0	0	0.0	1	2.0				
		INTERNATIONAL PROCEDURES (INT)																
INT	4300	INTL OSA	B,R		A	1	(N*)	730						3.0	4001		3100,3200,2201,2401,2300-N,4301,4100	
INT	4301	INTL ALS	B,R		A	1	(N*)	730						3.0	4001		3100,3200,2201,2401,2300-N,4300,4100	
		TOTAL INT STAGE							0	0.0	0	0.0	2	6.0				
		CORE PLUS TRAINING (3000 PHASE EVENTS) TOTAL							3	8.0	0	0.0	4	10.0				
		1000, 2000, 3000, & 4000 PHASE TOTAL							11	104	7	28.0	12	28.5				
		INSTRUCTOR TRAINING (5000 PHASE EVENTS)																
		INSTRUCTOR UNDER TRAINING (IUT)																
IUT	5100	INTRO FAM/INST MAN	B,R	E	A	1	D	*						2.0	6402	RS		
IUT	5101	PRAC FAM/INST MAN	B,R	E	A	1	D	*						2.0	5100	RS-opt		
IUT	5102	INSTRUCTIONAL TECHNIQUES	B,R	E	A	1	D	*						2.0	5101			
IUT	5103	IUT EVAL	B,R	E	A	1	D	*						2.0	5102	RS		

Enclosure (1)

UC-12W PILOT T&R MATRIX

STAGE	TRNG CODE	T&R DESCRIPTION	POI	DEVICE E	# OF A/C	CON	RE FLY	# OF ACAD	ACAD TIME	# OF SIM	SIM TIME	# OF FLTS	FLT TIME	PREREQUISITE	NOTES	CHAINING	EVENT CONV
		TOTAL IUT STAGE		E				0	0.0	0	0.0	4	8.0				
		INSTRUCTOR TRAINING (5000 PHASE EVENTS) TOTAL						0	0.0	0	0.0	4	8.0				
		REQUIREMENT, QUALIFICATIONS, AND DESIGNATIONS (RQD) (6000 PHASE)															
		RQD ACADEMICS (ACAD)															
ACAD	6000	NATOPS Open Book Exam	B,R	E			365		4.0								
ACAD	6001	NATOPS Closed Book Exam	B,R	E			365		2.0					6000			
ACAD	6002	NATOPS Oral Exam	B,R	E			365		2.0					6000, 6001			
ACAD	6003	Instrument Ground School	B,R	E			365		8.0								
ACAD	6004	Instrument Exam	B,R	E			365		2.0					6003			
ACAD	6005	Instrument Oral Exam	B,R	E			365		2.0					6004			
ACAD	6006	CRM BASIC	B,R	E			365		1.0								
ACAD	6007	CRM T/M/S	B,R	E			365		1.0								
ACAD	6008	FCP RESPONSIBILITIES	B,R	E			365		2.0								
ACAD	6009	Monthly EP Exam	B,R	E			30		1.0								
		TOTAL ACAD STAGE						2	3.0	0	0.0	0	0.0				
		NATOPS															
NATOPS	6100	NATOPS Evaluation	B,R	E	A/S	1 (N*)	365				0.0		2.0	6000, 6001, 6002, 2000 Phase Complete, 8200-8250			
NATOPS	6103	Quarterly EP Eval	B,R	E	A	1 (N*)	90						0.0		STATIC A/C		
		NATOPS TOTAL						0	0.0	0	0.0	2	2.0				
		INSTRUMENT (INST)															
INST	6101	Standard Instrument Eval	B,R	E	A/S	1 (N*)	355						2.0	2500, 6004, 6005		6101	
INST	6102	Special Instrument Eval	B,R	E	A/S	1 (N*)	365						2.0	2500, 6004, 6005			
		TOTAL INST STAGE						0	0.0	0	0.0	2	4.0				
		TRANSPORT 2 PILOT (T2P)															
T2P	6300	T2P UPGRADE	B,R	E	A	1	D	365					1.5	2000 Phase complete			
		TOTAL T2P STAGE						0	0.0	0	0.0	1	1.5				
		TRANSPORT AIRCRAFT COMMANDER (TAC)															
TAC	6400	Mission Proc Rev	B	E	A	1 (N*)	*						1.5	6300, 3000 Phase complete			

UC-12W PILOT T&R MATRIX

STAGE	TRNG CODE	T&R DESCRIPTION	POI	DEVICE E	DEVICE A	# OF A/C	CON	RE FLY	# OF ACAD	ACAD TIME	# OF SIM	SIM TIME	# OF FLTS	FLT TIME	PREREQUISITE	NOTES	CHAINING	EVENT CONV
TAC	6401	TAC REV	B	E	A	1	D	*						1.5	6400			
TAC	6402	TAC EVAL	B,R	E	A	1	D	365						2.0	6000,6001,6002,6401, 3000 Phase complete			
		TOTAL TAC STAGE							0	0.0	0	0.0	3	5.0				

FUNCTIONAL CHECK PILOT (FCP)

STAGE	TRNG CODE	T&R DESCRIPTION	POI	DEVICE E	DEVICE A	# OF A/C	CON	RE FLY	# OF ACAD	ACAD TIME	# OF SIM	SIM TIME	# OF FLTS	FLT TIME	PREREQUISITE
FCP	6500	FCP REVIEW	B	E	A	1	D	*						3.5	5103,6402,6008
FCP	6501	FCP EVAL	B,R	E	A	1	D	*						3.5	6500
		TOTAL FAC STAGE							0	0.0	0	0.0	2	7.0	

AVIATION CAREER PROGRESSION MODEL (ACPM)

STAGE	TRNG CODE	T&R DESCRIPTION	RE FLY	ACAD TIME	PREREQUISITE
ACPM	8200	MACCS AGENCIES, FUNCTIONS AND CONTROL OF AIRCRAFT AND MISSLES	*	0.6	2000 PHASE
ACPM	8201	MWCS BRIEF	*	0.4	2000 PHASE
ACPM	8202	ACA AND AIRSPACE	*	0.5	2000 PHASE
ACPM	8210	AVIATION GROUND SUPPORT	*	0.6	2000 PHASE
ACPM	8230	ACE BATTLESTAFF	*	0.6	2000 PHASE
ACPM	8231	BATTLE COMMAND DISPLAY	*	0.3	2000 PHASE
ACPM	8240	SIX FUNCTIONS OF MARINE AVIATION	*	1.3	2000 PHASE
ACPM	8241	JTAR/ASR INTRODUCTION AND PRACTICAL APPLICATION CLASS	*	0.5	2000 PHASE
ACPM	8242	SITE COMMAND PRIMER	*	0.7	2000 PHASE
ACPM	8250	THEATER AIR GROUND SYSTEM (TAGS)	*	0.6	2000 PHASE
ACPM	8300	AIR DEFENSE	*	0.6	3000 PHASE
ACPM	8310	FORWARD ARMING AND REFUELING POINT (FARP) OPERATIONS	*	0.4	3000 PHASE
ACPM	8311	MARINE CORPS TACTICAL FUEL SYSTEMS	*	0.2	3000 PHASE
ACPM	8320	JOINT STRUCTURE & JOINT AIR OPERATIONS	*	1.3	3000 PHASE

UC-12W PILOT T&R MATRIX

STAGE	TRNG CODE	T&R DESCRIPTION	POI	E	DEVICE	# OF A/C	CON	RE FLY	# OF ACAD	ACAD TIME	# OF SIM	SIM TIME	# OF FLTS	FLT TIME	PREREQUISITE	NOTES	CHAINING	EVENT CONV
ACPM	8321	JOINT AIR TASKING CYCLE PHASE 1: STRATEGY DEVELOPMENT						*		0.3					3000 PHASE			
ACPM	8322	JOINT AIR TASKING CYCLE PHASE 2: TARGET DEVELOPMENT						*		0.2					3000 PHASE			
ACPM	8323	JOINT AIR TASKING CYCLE PHASE 3: WEAPONING AND ALLOCATION						*		0.2					3000 PHASE			
ACPM	8324	JOINT AIR TASKING CYCLE PHASE 4: JOINT ATO PRODUCTION						*		0.2					3000 PHASE			
ACPM	8325	JOINT AIR TASKING CYCLE PHASE 5:						*		0.2					3000 PHASE			
ACPM	8326	JOINT AIR TASKING CYCLE PHASE 6: COMBAT ASSESSMENT						*		0.2					3000 PHASE			
ACPM	8340	INTEGRATING FIRES AND AIRSPACE WITHIN THE MAGTF						*		0.5					3000 PHASE			
ACPM	8350	PHASING CONTROL ASHORE						*		0.5					3000 PHASE			
ACPM	8351	TACRON ORGANIZATIONS AND FUNCTIONS						*		TBD					3000 PHASE			
ACPM	8630	TACTICAL AIR COMMAND CENTER (TACC)						*		0.7					6000 PHASE			
ACPM	8660	JOINT OPS INTRO						*		0.4					6000 PHASE			
ACPM	8640	JOINT DATA NETWORK						*		0.4					6000 PHASE			
ACPM	8641	MAGTF THEATER						*		1.5					6000 PHASE			
ACPM	8620	ESG/CSG INTEGRATION						*		TBD					6000 PHASE			
		TOTAL ACPM STAGE							28	13.9	0	0.0	0	0.0				

CHAPTER 3

UC-12W TRANSPORT AIRCREWMAN (TA)/6244

CHAPTER 3

UC-12W TRANSPORT AIRCREWMAN (TA)/6244

300. UC-12W TRANSPORT AIRCREWMAN (TA)/6244 INDIVIDUAL TRAINING AND READINESS
REQUIREMENTS. This T&R syllabus is based on specific goals and performance
standards designed to ensure individual proficiency in Core, Mission and Core
Plus Skills. The goal of this chapter is to develop individual and unit war
fighting capabilities.

301. UC-12W TRANSPORT AIRCREWMAN TRAINING PROGRESSION MODEL. This model
represents the recommended training progression for the average UC-12W
Transport Aircrewman crewmember. Units should use the model as a guide to
generate individual training plans.

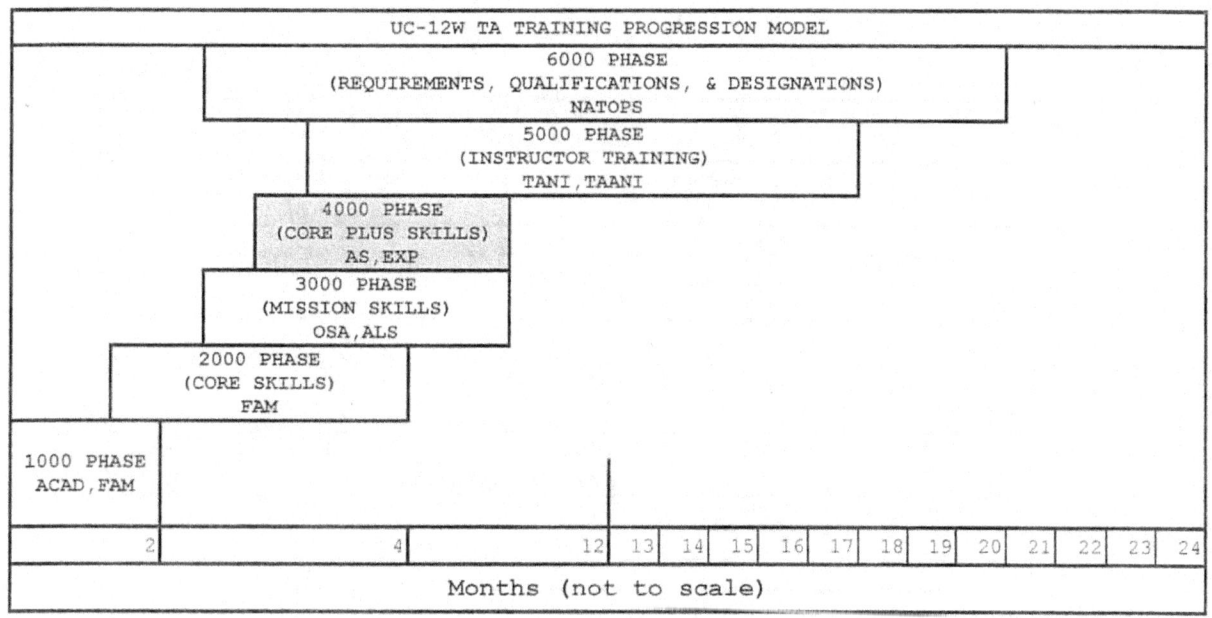

302. INDIVIDUAL CORE SKILL PROFICIENCY (CSP) REQUIREMENTS. A CSP crew
consists of individuals representing each crew position who have achieved and
currently maintain individual CSP. In order to be considered proficient in a
Core Skill, an individual must attain and maintain proficiency in Core Skill
events as delineated in the below paragraphs.

1. Events Required to Attain Individual CSP. To initially attain CSP in a
Core Skill, an individual must simultaneously have a proficient status in all
of the Core (2000 Phase) T&R events listed in the table below for that Core
Skill.

INDIVIDUAL CORE SKILL PROFICIENCY (CSP) ATTAIN TABLE
UC-12W Transport Aircrewman
FAM
2100R
2101R
Gray highlight & an R suffix on the event code = Refresher POI

2. Events Required to Maintain Individual CSP. To maintain CSP in a Core Skill, an individual must maintain proficiency in all 2000 phase T&R events listed for that Core Skill:

INDIVIDUAL CORE SKILL PROFICIENCY (CSP) MAINTAIN TABLE
UC-12W Transport Aircrewman
FAM
2101R
Gray highlight & an R suffix on the event code = Refresher POI

303. INDIVIDUAL MISSION SKILL PROFICIENCY (MSP) REQUIREMENTS. A MSP crew consists of individuals representing each crew position who have achieved and currently maintain Individual MSP. To be considered proficient in a Mission Skill, an individual must attain and maintain proficiency in Mission Skill events as delineated in the below paragraphs.

1. Events Required to Attain Individual MSP. To initially attain MSP in a Mission Skill, an individual must simultaneously have a proficient status in all 3000 phase T&R events listed for that Mission Skill:

INDIVIDUAL MISSION SKILL PROFICIENCY (MSP) ATTAIN TABLE	
UC-12W Transport Aircrewman	
T&R events required to Attain MSP (3000 Phase)	
OSA	ALS
3100R	3200R
Gray highlight & an R suffix on the event code = Refresher POI	

2. Events Required to Maintain Individual MSP. To maintain MSP in a Mission Skill, an individual must maintain proficiency in all 3000 phase T&R events listed for that Mission Skill:

INDIVIDUAL MISSION SKILL PROFICIENCY (MSP) MAINTAIN TABLE	
UC-12W Transport Aircrewman	
T&R events required to Maintain MSP (3000 Phase)	
OSA	ALS
3100R	3200R
Gray highlight & an R suffix on the event code = Refresher POI	

304. INDIVIDUAL CORE PLUS SKILL/MISSION PLUS SKILL PROFICIENCY REQUIREMENTS

1. Events Required to Attain Individual Proficiency in Core Plus Skills and Mission Plus Skills. Proficiency in Core Plus Skills/Mission Plus Skills is not required to obtain unit CSP. Training to Core Plus Skills/Mission Plus Skills is at the discretion of the unit commanding officer. To initially attain proficiency in a Core Plus Skill/Mission Plus Skill, an individual must simultaneously have a proficient status in all T&R events listed for that Core Plus Skill/Mission Plus Skill.

INDIVIDUAL CORE PLUS SKILL PROFICIENCY ATTAIN TABLE	
UC-12W Transport Aircrewman	
T&R events required to Attain Core Plus Proficiency (4000 Phase) Mission Plus	
AS	EXP
4100R	4200R
Gray highlight & an R suffix on the event code = Refresher POI	

2. Events Required to Maintain Individual Proficiency in Core Plus Skills and Mission Plus Skills. To maintain proficiency in a Core Plus

Skill/Mission Plus Skill, an individual must maintain proficiency in all T&R events listed in the table below for that Core Plus Skill Mission Plus:

INDIVIDUAL CORE PLUS SKILL PROFICIENCY MAINTAIN TABLE UC-12W Transport Aircrewman	
T&R events required to Maintain Core Plus Proficiency (4000 Phase) Mission Plus	
AS	EXP
4100R	4200R
Gray highlight & an R suffix on the event code = Refresher POI	

305. CERTIFICATION, QUALIFICATION AND DESIGNATION TABLES. The tables below delineate T&R events required to be completed to attain proficiency, initial qualifications and designations. In addition to event requirements, all required stage lectures, briefs, squadron training, prerequisites, and other criteria shall be completed prior to completing final events. Certification, qualification and designation letters signed by the commanding officer shall be placed in Aircrew Performance Records (APR) and NATOPS. Loss of proficiency in all qualification events causes the associated qualification to be lost. Regaining a qualification requires completing all R-coded syllabus events associated with that qualification.

INDIVIDUAL DESIGNATION REQUIREMENTS UC-12W Transport Aircrewman	
Designation	Initial Event Designation Requirements
TA	6100
TANI	5100,5101,5102
TAANI	5100,5101,5102

INDIVIDUAL QUALIFICATION REQUIREMENTS UC-12W Transport Aircrewman	
Qualification	Initial Event Qualification Requirements
NATOPS	6000,6001,6002,6100
CRM	6003

306. PROGRAMS OF INSTRUCTION (POI)

1. General

a. The time required to train a UC-12W Transport Aircrewman to completion of the Core Plus Phase is based off of flight hour requirements that are published in the UC-12W NATOPS manual. Assignment to a specific POI is determined by previous Aircrew experience. Transport Aircrewman Under Instruction (TAUI) without prior Naval Aircrew experience shall be assigned to the Basic (B) POI and shall continue to fly 2000 Phase level codes until the minimum flight hour requirement as delineated in NAVAIR 1A-C12WA-NFM-000 is met. TANI who were previously designated Naval Aircrew shall be assigned to the Basic (B) POI and may be designated as UC-12W TA upon successful completion of the Basic (B) POI. Those Aircrewman who were previously designated a UC-12W TA and are returning to a VMR shall be assigned to the Refresher (R) POI. When a crewmember completes a stage of training, that crewmember needs only to maintain proficiency in the (R) coded events for that stage to remain proficient.

b. All 1000 Phase level codes shall be instructed by a TANI. TAUI who are flying their 2000 Phase level codes to obtain their minimum flight hour requirement may fly with a qualified TA, TANI, or any qualified Pilot. 3000

Phase Level codes may be flown in place of 2000 level codes to obtain minimum flight hour requirements but shall be flown with a TANI.

2. Basic (B) POI. Basic (B) Transport Aircrewman shall fly the entire syllabus.

WEEKS	COURSE	PERFORMING ACTIVITY
1-3	Core Skill Introduction Training	VMR Det
4-8	Core Skill Training	VMR Det
8-12	Mission Skill Training	VMR Det
13-26	Core Plus Training	VMR Det

3. Refresher (R) POI. Refresher Transport Aircrewman shall fly those events annotated with a R. Commanding officers/OICs will review the qualifications, previous experience, currency, and demonstrated ability of Refresher Transport Aircrewman with a view towards combining required flights.

WEEKS	COURSE	PERFORMING ACTIVITY
1-2	Core Skill Introduction Training	VMR Det
3-6	Core Skill Training	VMR Det
7-12	Mission Skill Training	VMR Det
13-26	Core Plus Training	VMR Det

307. CORE SKILL INTRODCUTION (1000 PHASE)

1. General

    a. Core Skill Introduction training for the UC-12W is conducted at the squadron/unit.

    b. The purpose is to introduce Transport Aircrewman Under Instruction (TAUI) to the UC-12W. The focus shall be on Aircraft systems, handling, servicing, inspections and logistics.

    c. All events in the Core Skill Introduction phase shall be evaluated and documented by a TANI. The Syllabus Sponsor shall ensure standardization of all TANIs.

    d. Event completion is predicated upon demonstrated proficiency. When an individual successfully accomplishes the requirements of an event per the performance standards, the individual should log completion of the event (enter the appropriate T&R code) in M-SHARP. When the event is entered into M-SHARP, the individual's proficiency date for that event is automatically updated to reflect the date the event was completed. When supervising individual events, unit instructors/leaders shall ensure that trainees demonstrate proficiency per T&R standards prior to logging successful event completion. Evaluating individual proficiency in an event normally requires both objective and subjective assessment. If an individual fails to accomplish the requirements of an event per the performance standards, the individual should not log that event and the proficiency status for that event remains unchanged. Times indicated for each event are for planning purposes only.

    e. TAUIs shall fly events annotated with an N at least 30 minutes after official sunset. Events shall be flown in accordance with environmental conditions listed in the matrix below:

ENVIRONMENTAL CONDITIONS	
Code	Meaning
D	Shall be flown during hours of daylight: (by exception - there is no use of a symbol)
N*	Shall be flown during hours of darkness must be flown unaided
(N*)	May be flown during hours of darkness - If flown during hours of darkness must be flown unaided

2. Academic Ground School (ACAD)(1000 PHASE)

ACAD-1000   3.0   *   B   CLRM/1 UC-12W (Static)

> Goal. Introduce ground procedures, and aircraft systems.

> Requirements. Discuss aircraft mission, qualification requirements, CRM, aircraft publications, flight publications, flight schedule, flight advisory, NAVFLIR, Logbooks, M-Sharp. Discuss ICS/Radio procedures. Discuss aircraft weight limitations, center of gravity limitations, weight and balance terms and definitions, fuel imbalance limitations and baggage loading.

> Performance Standard. After introduction of above listed items, demonstrate understanding of each subject.

> External Syllabus Support. Static aircraft with ground power unit.

ACAD-1001   3.0   *   B   .   CLRM/1 UC-12W (Static)

> Goal. Introduce ground procedures, and aircraft systems.

> Requirements. Introduce Flight line safety, aircraft danger areas. Introduce aircraft discrepancy book, contract maintenance personnel, general aircraft description, UC-12W aircraft differences, preflight, aircraft security, and aircraft parking. Introduce radio procedures, aircraft fueling, engine oil servicing procedures. Introduce safety equipment, fire bottle location, survival equipment, ASE equipment and use, primary and emergency exit, O2 masks, egress, lavatory, coffee station, cabin preparation for flight, and seat operation. Review baggage loading.

> Performance Standard. After introduction of above listed items, demonstrate understanding of each subject.

> External Syllabus Support. Static aircraft with ground power unit.

3. Familiarization (FAM)

   a. Purpose. Introduce Transport Aircrewman to UC-12W FAM and CRM procedures.

   b. Crew Requirements. Shall be instructed/evaluated by a TANI.

FAM-1100   2.0   *   B   D   A   1 UC-12W

Goal. Introduce Operation of UC-12W aircraft.

Requirements. Introduce aircrew coordination/situational awareness. Perform Weight and Balance; and aircrew brief. Introduce normal and emergency checklist, flight packet, communication during critical phases of flight, lookout doctrine crew coordination, icing considerations, aircraft lighting, basic cockpit familiarization, and duties during an emergency. Introduce over the wing refueling procedures. Introduce preflight and post-flight inspections.

Performance Standard. After introduction of above listed items, demonstrate understanding of each subject.

Prerequisite. 1000, 1001

FAM-1101   2.0   *   B   D   A   1 UC-12W

Goal. Familiarization with aircraft systems and emergency procedures.

Requirements. Familiarize TAUI with aircrew coordination and situational awareness. Perform Weight and Balance and aircrew brief. Familiarize normal and emergency checklist, flight packet, communication during critical phases of flight, lookout doctrine crew coordination, icing considerations, aircraft lighting, basic cabin operations, and duties during an emergency. Familiarize over the wing refueling procedures at civil airfields, and familiarize preflight and post-flight inspections.

Performance Standard. After introduction of above listed items, demonstrate understanding of each subject.

Prerequisite. 1100

FAM-1102   2.0   *   B   N*   A   1 UC-12W

Goal. Familiarization with aircraft systems and emergency procedures during night operations.

Requirements. Familiarize TAUI with nighttime aircrew coordination/situational awareness. Perform Weight and Balance and aircrew brief. Familiarize TAUI with normal and emergency checklist, flight packet, communication during critical phases of flight, lookout doctrine crew coordination. Discuss night time considerations, icing considerations, aircraft lighting, basic cockpit orientation, and duties during an emergency. Familiarize TAUI with over the wing refueling procedures at civil airfields at night, familiarize preflight and post-flight inspections.

Performance Standard. After introduction of above listed items, demonstrate understanding of each subject.

Prerequisite. 1101

308. CORE SKILL (2000 PHASE)

1. General

   a. Purpose. Familiarize the TAUI with the Operational Support Aircraft mission. The TAUI shall continue to fly these codes under actual or simulated conditions until minimum flight hour requirement is met IAW NAVAIR 1A-C12WA-NFM-000.

2. Familiarization (FAM)

   a. Purpose. Introduce TAUIs to UC-12W FAM and CRM procedures.

   b. Crew Requirements. Shall be instructed/evaluated by an NI/ANI.

FAM-2100   2.0   *   B,R   (N*)   A   1 UC-12W

   Goal. Familiarization with Aircraft systems and radio operation.

   Requirements. Familiarize TAUI in the operation of aircraft systems to include pressurization and communications to include passenger phone system. Practice normal procedures and simulated emergency procedures.

   Performance Standard. After introduction of above listed items, demonstrate understanding and operation of each subject.

   Prerequisite. 1102

FAM-2101   2.0   365   B,R   (N*)   A   1 UC-12W

   Goal. Familiarization with DV passenger procedures.

   Requirements. Familiarize TAUI with DV passenger procedures under simulated conditions. Discuss military appearance, customs and courtesies. DV Passenger comfort, baggage handling, passenger manifest, and passenger safety. Perform passenger brief.

   Performance Standard. After introduction of above listed items, demonstrate understanding of each subject.

   Prerequisite. 2100

309. MISSION SKILL (3000 PHASE)

1. General

   a. Purpose. Familiarize the TAUI with the Operational Support Aircraft mission. The TAUI shall continue to fly these codes under actual or simulated conditions until minimum flight hour requirement is met in accordance with NAVAIR 1A-C12WA-NFM-000

   b. Crew Requirements. Shall be instructed/evaluated by a TANI.

2. Operational Support Airlift (OSA)

OSA-3100   2.0   60   B,R   (N*)   A   1 UC-12W

   Goal. Conduct an Operational Support Airlift (OSA) Mission.

   Requirements. Conduct OSA mission: Crew coordination, fuel requirements, weight and balance, baggage handling, passenger comfort and safety, RON, normal and emergency procedures, passenger brief.

Performance Standard. Conduct flight IAW NAVAIR 1A-C12WA-NFM-000. Assist pilots as required with all normal and emergency procedures.

Prerequisite. 2000 PHASE Complete

3. Air Logistics Support ALS

ALS-3200   2.0   60   B,R   (N*)   A   1 UC-12W

Goal. Conduct an Air Logistics Support (ALS) Mission.

Requirements. Conduct ALS mission: Crew coordination, fuel requirements, weight and balance, cargo certification and handling, special cargo considerations, RON, normal and emergency procedures.

Performance Standard. Conduct flight IAW NAVAIR 1A-C12WA-NFM-000. Assist pilots as required with all normal and emergency procedures.

Prerequisite. 2000 PHASE Complete

310. CORE PLUS (4000 PHASE)

1. General

   a. The Core Plus Phase consists of academics, skill, and mission training.

   b. Core Plus training is defined as theater specific and/or low likelihood of occurrence training and should not be the focus of unit training.

2. Core Plus Academics (ACAD)

ACAD-4000   2.0   *   B,R   CLRM

General. At the publishing date of this manual, the ASE academic period of instruction is under development by the Syllabus Sponsor (VMR Det Bell Chase) and it will be distributed to the UC-12W community once completed. Not sure if this applies to TA.

3. Assault Support (AS)

AS-4100   2.0   730   B,R   (N*)   A   1 UC-12W

General. At the publishing date of this manual, the AS flight is under development by the Syllabus Sponsor (VMR Det Andrews) and it will be distributed to the UC-12W community once completed. Not sure if this applies to TA.

4. Expeditionary Shore-Based Operations (EXP)

EXP-4200   2.0   730   B,R   (N*)   A   1 UC-12W

Goal. Conduct unimproved runway operations.

Requirements. Conduct aviation operations when deployed OCONUS. This event should be logged in conjunction with OAS-3100 or ALS-3200 when performed during contingency operations.

Performance Standard. Conduct flight IAW NAVAIR 1A-C12WA-NFM-000and Theatre specific SPINS.

Prerequisite. 3000 Phase complete, 4000

311. INSTRUCTOR TRAINING (5000 PHASE)

1. General. The Instructor Phase consists of three events leading to the Transport Aircrewman NATOPS Instructor and Transport Aircrewman Assistant NATOPS Designations.

2. Instructor Under Training (IUT)

IUT-5100   2.0   *   B,R   D   E   A   1 UC-12W

Goal. TA NATOPS Instructor Familiarization.

Requirements. Introduce the TANI under instruction (UI) to the skills required to correct common errors and prepare the TANI(UI) to conduct T&R syllabus and NATOPS evaluation flights. Discuss Instructional techniques and conducting a NATOPS Evaluation. Review passenger procedures, night considerations, icing considerations, weight and balance, aircraft servicing and emergency procedures.

Performance Standard. After introduction of above listed item, demonstrate understanding of each subject.

Prerequisite. Designated TA

IUT-5101   2.0   *   B,R   (N*)   E   A   1 UC-12W

Goal. TA NATOPS Instructor Review.

Requirements. Review passenger manifest, passenger briefing, passenger procedures, DV procedures, special cargo, aircraft handling, fueling, all weather operations and RON procedures. Discuss environmental system, pressurization system, oxygen system, and aircraft lighting. Practice preflight and postflight, checklists, all normal and emergency procedures, TA duties and responsibilities.

Performance Standard. Demonstrate satisfactory knowledge of passenger handling procedures and passenger brief. Assist pilots as required with all normal and emergency procedures.

Prerequisite. 5100

IUT-5102   2.0   *   B,R   (N*)   E   A   1 UC-12W

Goal. TANI/ANI designation evaluation flight.

Requirements. TANI(UI) is to brief and conduct a NATOPS evaluation on the TANI. TANI(UI) must show a thorough knowledge of all academic and flight requirements of a Transport Aircrewman and demonstrate the ability to instruct a student on the requirements.

Performance Standard. Demonstrate a thorough knowledge of and be able to effectively instruct all aircraft systems, limitations, normal and emergency procedures, and TA responsibilities.

Prerequisite. 5101

312. REQUIREMENTS, QUALIFICATIONS, DESIGNATIONS (RQD) (6000 PHASE)

1. UC-12W RQD Academics (ACAD)

ACAD-6000   4.0   365   B,R   E   NATOPs Open Book

> Goal. The open book examination shall consist of, but not be
> limited to the question bank found in the 1A-C12WA-NFM-000. The
> purpose of the open book examination is to evaluate the TA's
> knowledge of the appropriate publications and the aircraft.

> Performance Standard. Achieve a minimum score of 3.5 on the open
> book examination.

ACAD-6001   2.0   365   B,R   E   NATOPS Closed Book

> Goal. The purpose of the closed book is to evaluate the TA's
> knowledge of normal and emergency procedures and aircraft
> limitations.

> Performance Standard. Achieve a minimum score of 3.3 on the
> closed book examination.

ACAD-6002   2.0   365   B,R   E   NATOPS Oral

> Goal. The oral examination shall consist of, but not be limited
> to the question bank found in the 1A-C12WA-NFM-000. The
> instructor may draw upon their own experience to ask questions of
> a direct and objective nature to evaluate the TA's knowledge of
> normal and emergency procedures and aircraft limitations.

> Performance Standard. Achieve a minimum grade of qualified on
> the oral examination.

> Prerequisite. 6000, 6001

ACAD-6003   2.0   365   B,R   E   CRM BASIC

> Goal. This course of instruction is under development by VMR Det
> Belle Chase and will be distributed to the UC-12W community once
> completed.

> Requirements.

ACAD-6004   1.0   365   B,R   E   CRM UC-12W

> Goal. This course of instruction is under development by VMR Det
> Belle Chase, LA and will be distributed to the UC-12W community
> once completed.

ACAD-6005   1.0   30   B,R   E   Monthly EP Exam

> Goal. Successfully complete the UC-12W Monthly Emergency
> Procedures Examination.

> Requirement. Pass the Monthly Emergency Procedures Examination.

> Performance Standard. Achieve a passing score on the Monthly
> Emergency Procedures Examination.

2. NATOPS Evaluation

NTPS-6100   2.0   365   B,R   (N*)   E   A   1 UC-12W

Goal. Complete annual NATOPS flight evaluation. Conduct an evaluation of the TA's knowledge of mission and normal operating procedures (flight and ground), CRM, aircraft systems, emergency procedures.

Requirements. Demonstrate a comprehensive knowledge and understanding of NATOPS, and SOP.

Performance Standard. Achieve a minimum grade of qualified on the evaluation.

Prerequisite. 6000, 6001, 6002, 6003

NTPS-6101   0.0   90   B,R   (N*)   E   A   1 UC-12W Static

Goal. Quarterly NATOPS static aircraft emergency procedures review.

Requirement. This review should cover selected aircraft emergencies in a static aircraft. This event can be completed in conjunction with a flight. Demonstrate comprehensive knowledge and understanding of NATOPS emergencies.

Performance Standard. Executes the review in accordance with NATOPS.

Performance Standard. Executes flight and ground operations safely IAW OPNAV 3710.7, NATOPS, NATOPS Instrument Flight Manual, and training rules.

Prerequisite. Meets OPNAVINST 3710.7 Special Instrument requirements, recommended by Stan Board, 6003, 6004, 6005

313. UC-12W TRANSPORT AIRCREWMAN (TA) T&R SYLLABUS MATRIX

UC-12W TA T&R MATRIX

STAGE	TRNG CODE	T&R DESCRIPTION	POI	DEVICE E	# OF A/C	CON	RE FLY	# OF ACAD	ACAD TIME	# OF SIM	SIM TIME	# OF FLTS	FLT TIME	PREREQUISITE	NOTES	CHAINING	EVENT CONV
CORE SKILL INTRODUCTION TRAINING (1000 PHASE EVENTS)																	
CORE SKILL ACADEMICS																	
ACAD	1000	GROUND PROCEDURES	B				*		3.0								
ACAD	1001	AIRCRAFT SYSTEMS	B				*		3.0								
TOTAL CORE SKILL INTRODUCTION ACADEMICS								2	6.0	0	0.0	0	0.0				
FAMILIARIZATION (FAM)																	
FAM	1100	INTRO UC-12W	B	A	1	D	*						2.0	1000,1001			
FAM	1101	A/C SYSTEMS EPs	B	A	1	D	*						2.0	1100			
FAM	1102	NIGHT FAM	B	A	1	N*	*						2.0	1101			
TOTAL FAM STAGE								0	0.0	0	0.0	3	6.0				
CORE SKILL INTRODUCTION TRAINING (1000 PHASE EVENTS) TOTAL								2	6.0	0	0.0	3	6.0				
CORE SKILL TRAINING (2000 PHASE EVENTS)																	
FAMILIARIZATION (FAM)																	
FAM	2100	A/C SYSTEMS & RADIOS	B,R	A	1	(N*)	*						2.0	1102			
FAM	2101	INTRO DV PROCEDURES	B,R	A	1	(N*)	365						2.0	2100			
TOTAL FAM STAGE								0	0.0	0	0.0	2	4.0				
CORE SKILL TRAINING (2000 PHASE EVENTS) TOTAL								0	0.0	0	0.0	2	4.0				
MISSION SKILL TRAINING (3000 PHASE EVENTS)																	
OPERATIONAL SUPPORT AIRLIFT (OSA)																	
OSA	3100	OSA	B,R	A	1	(N*)	60						2.0	2000 Phase Complete	PAX	2101,3200	
TOTAL OSA STAGE								0	0.0	0	0.0	1	2.0				
AIR LOGISTICS SUPPORT (ALS)																	
ALS	3200	ALS	B,R	A	1	(N*)	60						2.0	2000 Phase Complete	CARGO	2101,3100	
TOTAL ALS STAGE								0	0.0	0	0.0	1	2.0				
TOTAL MISSION SKILL TRAINING (3000 PHASE EVENTS)								0	0.0	0	0.0	2	4.0				
CORE PLUS TRAINING (4000 PHASE EVENTS)																	
CORE PLUS ACADEMICS																	
ACAD	4000	ASE Academics	B,R				*	1	2.0								
TOTAL ACAD STAGE								1	2.0	0							
ASSAULT SUPPORT (AS)																	
AS	4100	TACTICAL PROCEDURES	B,R	A	1	(N*)	*						2.0	4000,2100	ASE	3100,3200,2101,4200	
TOTAL AS STAGE								0	0.0	0	0.0	1	2.0				
EXPEDITIONARY SHORE-BASED OPERATIONS (EXP)																	
EXP	4200	EXP OPERATIONS	B,R	A	1	(N*)	*						2.0	3000 Phase complete,4000		3100,3200,2101	
TOTAL EXP STAGE								0	0.0	0	0.0	1	2.0				
CORE PLUS TRAINING (4000 PHASE EVENTS) TOTAL								1	2.0	0	0.0	2	4.0				
2000, 3000, & 4000 PHASE TOTAL								1	2.0	0	0.0	6	12.0				

3-14

UC-12W TA T&R MATRIX

STAGE	TRNG CODE	T&R DESCRIPTION	POI	DEVICE E	DEVICE A	# OF A/C	CON	RE FLY	# OF ACAD	ACAD TIME	# OF SIM	SIM TIME	# OF FLTS	FLT TIME	PREREQUISITE	NOTES	CHAINING	EVENT CONV
									INSTRUCTOR TRAINING (500 PHASE EVENTS)									
									INSTRUCTOR UNDER TRAINING (IUT)									
IUT	5100	INTRO FAM	B,R	E	A	1	D	*						2.0	Designation TA			
IUT	5101	INSTRUCTOR FAM	B,R	E	A	1	(N*)	*						2.0	5100			
IUT	5102	EVAL	B,R	E	A	1	(N*)	*						2.0	5101			
		TOTAL IUT STAGE							0	0.0	0	0.0	3	6.0				
		INSTRUCTOR TRAINING (5000 PHASE EVENTS) TOTAL							0	0.0	0	0.0	3	6.0				
								REQUIREMENT, QUALIFICATIONS, AND DESIGNATIONS (RQD) (6000 PHASE)										
								RQD ACADEMICS (ACAD)										
ACAD	6000	NATOPS Open Book Exam	B,R	E				365		4.0					6000			
ACAD	6001	NATOPS Closed Book	B,R	E				365		2.0					6000,6001			
ACAD	6002	NATOPS Oral Exam	B,R	E				365		2.0					6003			
ACAD	6003	CRM BASIC	B,R	E				365		2.0						ACAD 6003		
ACAD	6004	CRM T/M/S	B,R	E				365		1.0					6003			
ACAD	6005	Monthly EP Exam	B,R	E				30		1.0								
		TOTAL ACAD STAGE							5	11.0	0	0.0	0	0.0				
								NATOPS										
NATOPS	6100	NATOPS Evaluation	B,R	E	A	1	(N*)	365					2	2.0	6000,6001,6002,6003			
NATOPS	6101	Quarterly EP Eval	B,R	E	A	A	(N*)	90										
		NATOPS TOTAL							0	0.0	0	0.0	2	2.0				

Enclosure (1)

CHAPTER 4

UC-12W QUALIFIED OBSERVER

CHAPTER 4

UC-12W QUALIFIED OBSERVER

400. UC-12W QUALIFIED OBSERVER INDIVIDUAL TRAINING AND READINESS
REQUIREMENTS. This T&R syllabus is based on specific goals and performance
standards designed to ensure individual proficiency in Core, Mission and Core
Plus Skills. The goal of this chapter is to develop individual and unit war
fighting capabilities.

401. UC-12W QUALIFIED OBSERVER TRAINING PROGRESSION MODEL. This model
represents the recommended training progression for the average UC-12W
Qualified Observer crewmember. Units should use the model as a guide to
generate individual training plans.

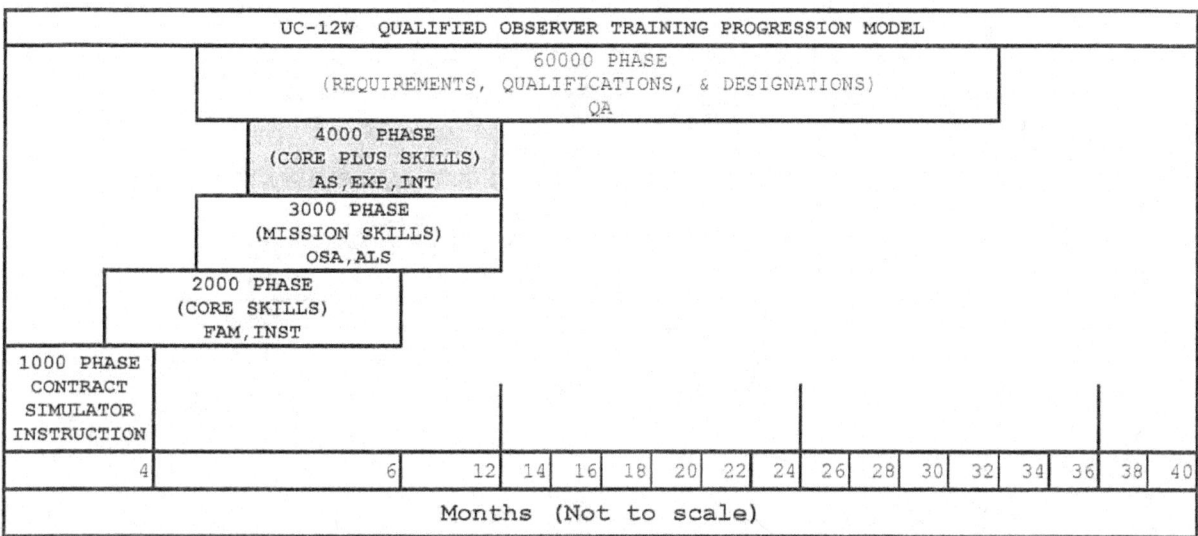

402. INDIVIDUAL CORE SKILL PROFICIENCY (CSP) REQUIREMENTS. A CSP crew
consists of individuals representing each crew position who have achieved and
currently maintain individual CSP. In order to be considered proficient in a
Core Skill, an individual must attain and maintain proficiency in Core Skill
events as delineated in the below paragraphs.

1. Events Required to Attain Individual CSP. To initially attain CSP in a
Core Skill, an individual must simultaneously have a proficient status in all
of the Core (2000 Phase) T&R events listed in the table below for that Core
Skill.

INDIVIDUAL CORE SKILL PROFICIENCY (CSP) ATTAIN TABLE UC-12W Qualified Observer	
T&R events required to Attain CSP (2000 Phase)	
FAM	INST
2100 2101R 2102R	2200R 2201R
Gray highlight & an R suffix on the event code = Refresher POI	
An S prefix on the event code = Event conducted in a simulator	

2. <u>Events Required to Maintain Individual CSP</u>. The QO has no event requirements to maintain in the Core level series.

403. <u>INDIVIDUAL MISSION SKILL PROFICIENCY (MSP) REQUIREMENTS</u>. A MSP crew consists of individuals representing each crew position who have achieved and currently maintain Individual MSP. To be considered proficient in a Mission Skill, an individual must attain and maintain proficiency in Mission Skill events as delineated in the below paragraphs.

1. <u>Events Required to Attain Individual MSP</u>. To initially attain MSP in a Mission Skill, an individual must simultaneously have a proficient status in all 3000 phase T&R events listed for that Mission Skill:

INDIVIDUAL MISSION SKILL PROFICIENCY (MSP) ATTAIN TABLE UC-12W Qualified Observer	
T&R events required to Attain MSP (3000 Phase)	
OSA	ALS
3100R	3200R
Gray highlight & an R suffix on the event code = Refresher POI	

2. <u>Events Required to Maintain Individual MSP</u>. To maintain MSP in a Mission Skill, an individual must maintain proficiency in all 3000 phase T&R events listed for that Mission Skill:

INDIVIDUAL MISSION SKILL PROFICIENCY (MSP) MAINTAIN TABLE UC-12W Qualified Observer	
T&R events required to Maintain MSP (3000 Phase)	
OSA	ALS
3100R	3200R
Gray highlight & an R suffix on the event code = Refresher POI	

404. <u>INDIVIDUAL CORE PLUS SKILL/MISSION PLUS SKILL PROFICIENCY REQUIREMENTS</u>

1. <u>Events Required to Attain Individual Proficiency in Core Plus Skills and Mission Plus Skills</u>. Proficiency in Core Plus Skills/Mission Plus Skills is not required to obtain unit CSP. Training to Core Plus Skills/Mission Plus Skills is at the discretion of the unit commanding officer. To initially attain proficiency in a Core Plus Skill/Mission Plus Skill, an individual must simultaneously have a proficient status in all T&R events listed for that Core Plus Skill/Mission Plus Skill.

INDIVIDUAL CORE PLUS SKILL PROFICIENCY ATTAIN TABLE UC-12W Qualified Observer		
T&R events required to Attain Core Plus Proficiency (4000 Phase)		
AS	EXP	INT
4100R	4200R	4300R
		4301R
Gray highlight & an R suffix on the event code = Refresher POI		

2. <u>Events Required to Maintain Individual Proficiency in Core Plus Skills and Mission Plus Skills</u>. To maintain proficiency in a Core Plus Skill/Mission Plus Skill, an individual must maintain proficiency in all T&R events listed in the table below for that Core Plus Skill Mission Plus Skill:

INDIVIDUAL CORE PLUS SKILL PROFICIENCY MAINTAIN TABLE UC-12W Qualified Observer		
T&R events required to Maintain Core Plus Proficiency (4000 Phase)		
AS	EXP	INT
4100R	4200R	4300R
		4301R
Gray highlight & an R suffix on the event code = Refresher POI		

405. <u>CERTIFICATION, QUALIFICATION AND DESIGNATION TABLE</u>. The table below delineate T&R events required to be completed to attain proficiency, initial

qualifications and designations. In addition to event requirements, all required stage lectures, briefs, squadron training, prerequisites, and other criteria shall be completed prior to completing final events. Certification, qualification and designation letters signed by the commanding officer shall be placed in Aircrew Performance Records (APR) and NATOPS. Loss of proficiency in all qualification events causes the associated qualification to be lost. Regaining a qualification requires completing all R-coded syllabus events associated with that qualification.

INDIVIDUAL DESIGNATION/QUALIFICATION REQUIREMENTS UC-12W Qualified Observer	
Designation / Qualification	Initial Event Designation Requirements
QO	6000,6001,6002,6003,6004,6005,6500
NATOPS	6000,6001,6002,6100
INSTRUMENT	6003,6004,6005
CRM	6006,6007

406. PROGRAMS OF INSTRUCTION (POI)

1. Basic (B) POI. Basic Qualified Observers shall fly the entire syllabus.

WEEKS	COURSE	PERFORMING ACTIVITY
4-6	Core Skill Introduction Training	CACT
2-6	Core Skill Training	VMR Det
2-6	Mission Skill Training	VMR Det

3. Refresher (R) POI. Refresher Qualified Observers shall fly those events annotated with an R. Commanding officers/OICs will review the qualifications, previous experience, currency, and demonstrated ability of Refresher Qualified Observers with a view towards combining required flights.

WEEKS	COURSE	PERFORMING ACTIVITY
4-6	Core Skill Introduction Training	CACT
2-6	Core Skill Training	VMR Det
2-6	Mission Skill Training	VMR Det

407. CORE SKILL INTRODUCTION PHASE (1000)

1. General

    a. Core Skill Introduction training for the UC-12W is conducted by a Command Aircraft Crew Training (CACT) facility. The UC-12W Syllabus Sponsor is responsible for contract negotiations and syllabus content/changes. Recommendations for CACT changes shall be submitted to the Syllabus Sponsor.

    b. All academic requirements for this phase of training are incorporated into the CACT course.

    c. All events in the Core Skill Introduction phase shall be evaluated and documented by a civilian instructor. The Syllabus Sponsor shall ensure standardization of civilian contracted instructors.

    d. Event completion is predicated upon demonstrated proficiency. When an individual successfully accomplishes the requirements of an event per the performance standards, the individual should log completion of the event (enter the appropriate T&R code) in M-SHARP. When the event is entered into M-SHARP, the individual's proficiency date for that event is automatically updated to reflect the date the event was completed. When supervising individual events, unit instructors/leaders shall ensure that trainees demonstrate proficiency per T&R standards prior to logging successful event completion. Evaluating individual proficiency in an event normally requires both objective and subjective assessment. If an individual fails to accomplish the requirements of an event per the performance standards, the individual should not log that event and the proficiency status for that event remains unchanged. Times indicated for each event are for planning purposes only.

e. While attending either the CACT approved QO Initial or QO Recurrent courses, the QOUI will spend 2 hours in the right seat for each sortie.

f. Every attempt should be made to ensure USMC checklists and procedures are studied and adhered to during the CACT training.

g. CACT INT SIM 1101 thru CACT INT SIM 1109 may be accomplished with just the QOUI and contracted instructor. However, every attempt should be made to pair the QOUI up with another USN/USMC PUI in order to facilitate training using established USN/USMC UC-12 procedures.

h. Qualified Observers shall fly events annotated with an N at least 30 minutes after official sunset. Events shall be flown in accordance with environmental conditions listed in the matrix below:

ENVIRONMENTAL CONDITIONS	
Code	Meaning
D	Shall be flown during hours of daylight: (by exception - there is no use of a symbol)
N*	Shall be flown during hours of darkness must be flown unaided
(N*)	May be flown during hours of darkness - If flown during hours of darkness must be flown unaided
Note - If the event is to be flown in the simulator the Simulator Instructor shall set the desired environmental conditions for the event.	

2. Command Aircraft Crew Training (CACT) Ground School

ACAD-1000   48.0   *   B   CLRM

Goal. CACT Initial Ground School: Aircraft Systems, CRM, Weight & Balance, Performance, flight planning, Windshear, EGPWS/CFIT, TCASII.

Requirements. Per current contract.

Performance Standard. Per current contract.

ACAD-1001   8.0   365   R   CLRM

Goal. CACT Recurrent Ground School.

Requirements. Per current contract.

Performance Standard. Per current contract.

Prerequisite. ACAD-1000

ACAD-1002   3.0   *   B   CLRM

Goal. RVSM.

Requirements. Per current contract.

Performance Standard. Per current contract.

ACAD-1003   2.0   365   B,R   CLRM

    Goal. Weather Radar.

    Requirements. Per current contract.

    Performance Standard. Per current contract.

ACAD-1004   21.0   *   B,R   CLRM

    Goal. CACT Initial International Procedures

    Requirements. Per current contract.

    Performance Standard. Per current contract.

ACAD-1005   8.0   730   R   CLRM

    Goal. CACT Recurrent International Procedures

    Requirements. Per current contract.

    Performance Standard. Per current contract.

    Prerequisite. ACAD-1004

3. Civilian Approved Contractor Training (CACT) Simulator Training

CACT-1101   2.0   *   B   (N*)   S

    Goal. Per current contract.

    Requirements. Per current contract.

    Performance Standard. Per current contract.

CACT-1102   2.0   *   B   (N*)   S

    Goal. Per current contract.

    Requirements. Per current contract.

    Performance Standard. Per current contract.

CACT-1103   2.0   *   B   (N*)   S

    Goal. Per current contract.

    Requirements. Per current contract.

    Performance Standard. Per current contract.

CACT-1104   2.0   *   B   (N*)   S

    Goal. Per current contract.

    Requirements. Per current contract.

    Performance Standard. Per current contract.

CACT-1105   2.0   365   B,R   (N*)   S

    Goal. Per current contract.

Enclosure (1)

Requirements. Per current contract.

Performance Standard. Per current contract.

CACT-1106   2.0   365   B,R   (N*)   S

Goal. Per current contract.

Requirements. Per current contract.

Performance Standard. Per current contract.

CACT-1107   2.0   365   B,R   (N*)   S

Goal. Per current contract.

Requirements. Per current contract.

Performance Standard. Per current contract.

408. CORE SKILL (2000 PHASE)

1. Core Skill Academic (ACAD)

    a. Purpose. Introduce the Qualified Observers to the UC-12W.

    b. General. The Qualified Observer should be CACT complete prior to beginning this stage.

ACAD-2000   3.0   *   B,R   D   A   1 UC-12W

Goal. Introduce the UC-12W aircraft.

Requirements

Brief: ADB, MEL/CDL, Chapter 29 Flight Crew Coordination, Pre-flight, Emergency Equipment, Egress Drill, Post Flight, M-Sharp, CP-CALC, Flight-planning, ORM, WX Brief, NOTAMS, Fuel Packet/Multi-use Card, OPARS, Short Field High Obstacle.

Performance Standard. After introduction of above listed items, demonstrate understanding of each subject.

External Syllabus Support. Static aircraft.

Prerequisite. 1101-1109

ACAD-2001   3.0   *   B,R   D   A   1 UC-12W

Goal. Introduce the UC-12W avionics and navigation systems on a powered aircraft.

Requirements. Demonstrate the power up, set up, and various functions of the FMS, radios and avionics.

Performance Standard. Show proficiency in the use of all navigation equipment and radios.

External Syllabus Support. Ground powered aircraft.

Prerequisite. 2000

2. Familiarization (FAM)

    a. Purpose. Introduce Qualified Observers to UC-12W FAM and CRM procedures.

b. General

(1) QOUIs shall successfully complete approved CACT initial course prior to starting this phase of training.

(2) Flights in this phase of instruction shall be flown sequentially, single-sortie, with complete brief/debrief for each flight.

(3) Only aircrew scheduled for CACT recurrent training shall complete the CACT INT SIM 1120 to CACT INT SIM 1122 series codes.

c. Crew Requirements. IP/QOUI.

FAM-2101   2.0   *   B   D   A   1 UC-12W

Goal. Introduce the UC-12W aircraft.

Requirements. Brief preflight/flight planning, aircrew coordination/voice calls, checklists, normal start procedures, abnormal starts, engine fire on deck, aborted takeoff, runaway torque on deck/in flight, emergency egress, taxiing, run-up (procedure & limits), takeoff, touch-and-go procedures, fuel system & emergencies, landing gear system and emergencies, and critical memory items. Discuss windshear as a hazard to flight, windshear recognition, avoidance and escape maneuver. Review preflight. Introduce checklists, communication procedures and equipment, demonstrate starting engines, taxi and engine run-up, normal takeoff, aborted takeoff, climb schedule (charts), normal cruise, slow flight, steep turns, approach to stall/full stalls, unusual attitudes, oxygen system, environmental control, and post flight. Observe landings (full flap, approach flap, no flap and with reverse), engine failure in flight and emergency engine shutdown, starter assisted air start, and wave off. Debrief.

Performance Standard. In accordance with NFM.

Prerequisite. 1000 Phase complete.

FAM-2102   2.0   *   B,R   D   A   1 UC-12W

Goal. Refine right seat procedures for ground and flight operations in VFR environment.

Requirements. Observe engine starts with associated failures and practice normal and abbreviated ground procedures. Review the charts and practice the procedures applicable to high altitude, high temperature takeoff with an engine failure after Vr, a subsequent single engine approach, and/or single engine missed approach. Review the pressurization system, pneumatic systems, environmental systems, oxygen system, and related malfunctions. Continue to review the engine system, propeller system, electrical system, fuel system, and related malfunctions. Conduct additional instrument procedures, approaches, and missed approaches. Observe crosswind landings, takeoffs, and recovery from low level wind shear. Continue to apply Aircrew Coordination skills.

Performance Standard. In accordance with NFM.

Prerequisite. 2101

3. Instruments (INST)

    a. Purpose. To acquaint the QOUI with the flight characteristics, navigation equipment, and flight instruments under simulated or actual instrument flying conditions. QOUI should demonstrate keen awareness of flight instrument interpretation and spatial orientation. After completion of stage, QOUI should be able to operate as a crewmember in the Air Traffic Control environment outside the local area.

    b. General. Approaches should terminate in touch-and-go landings, if possible, emphasizing Missed Approach Point/Decision Altitude decision making to either a normal landing or missed approach. Events should be flown with at least 1 approach and landing at an airfield other than the QOUI's home field.

    c. Crew Requirements. IP/QOUI.

    d. Ground/Academic Training. Complete locally approved Instrument Ground school course.

INST-2200   2.0   *   B   (N*)   A   1 UC-12W

                Goal. Introduce UC-12 navigation equipment and non-precision/precision approach capabilities.

                Requirements. Preflight briefing to include propeller system, bleed air system, explosive decompression, lost communications, fuselage fire, comm/nav radios, AP/FD use SID's & STAR's, en route ATC procedures, instrument approach procedures straight in approaches and circling approaches, weather radar, severe weather procedures. Discuss TCAS II system, warnings and conflict resolution. Review preflight, checklists, engine start hot start and no light-off, (taxi no brakes and hot brakes), abort, climb, cruise, engine shutdown, airstart, post flight, and M-SHARP. Introduce prop failure/overspeed, fuselage fire, engine chip light, fuel cross feed after engine failure, manual gear extension, emergency descent, landings (two engine and single engine), instrument approaches straight in and circling, TACAN, VOR, LOC BC, NDB, ASR, ILS and PAR, missed approach (dual engine and single engine), holding. Debrief.

                Performance Standard. In accordance with NATOPS Flight Manual, Chapter 7 (Shore-Based Procedures) and Chapter 18 (Instrument Flight Procedures).

                Prerequisite. 1000 Phase complete.

INST-2201   2.0   365   B,R   (N*)   A   1 UC-12W

                Goal. Introduce ProLine 21 instrument procedures and precision/non-precision capabilities.

                Requirements. Preflight briefing and flight to include NATOPS Part VI precision/non-precision/FMS approaches, limitations and requirements. Flight Level Change, Vs modes (Pitch/Vertical Velocity/Speed), VOR procedures, ILS/LOC/BC procedures, GCA/ASR procedures, RNAV procedures, TACAN procedures, autopilot/Flight Director Indicator (FDI)/Horizontal Situation Indicator (HSI) utilization, airspeed indicator operation and setup, en route/cruise procedures, and copilot/QO utilization/duties.

Introduce non-auto pilot instrument departure, VOR approach, ILS/LOC/BC approach, RNAV approaches, TACAN approach, ASR/GCA approach, holding, missed approach procedures and pilot/copilot crew coordination. Discuss volcanic ash hazard to flight, recognition and avoidance. Review normal landings, SSE landings, previous emergencies, and procedures.

Performance Standard. In accordance with NATOPS flight manual and NATOPS instrument flight manual.

Prerequisite. 2200

409. MISSION SKILL PHASE (3000)

1. General. All Mission Skill events shall be instructed by an NI or ANI.

2. Operational Support Airlift

OSA-3100   2.0   60   B,R   (N*)   A   1 UC-12W

Goal. Conduct an Operational Support Airlift (OSA) mission.

Requirements.

Brief: Mission and crew coordination, flight planning, weather, fuel requirements, weight and balance, aircraft performance factors, RON, passenger requirements, scheduling agency (JOSAC/MCB Japan) coordination, and emergency procedures.

Flight: Conduct an OSA mission.

Performance Standard. Demonstrate satisfactory knowledge of aircraft operating procedures and limitations.

Prerequisite. 2000 Phase complete, 6100, 6101.

3. Air Logistics Support

ALS-3200   2.0   60   B,R   (N*)   A   1 UC-12W

Goal. Conduct an Air Logistics Support (ALS) mission.

Requirements.

Brief: Mission and crew coordination, flight planning, weather, fuel requirements, weight and balance, aircraft performance factors, RON, scheduling agency (JOSAC, MCB JAPAN) coordination, cargo certification and handling, special cargo considerations, and emergency procedures.

Flight: Conduct an ALS mission.

Performance Standard. Demonstrate satisfactory knowledge of aircraft operating procedures and limitations.

Prerequisite. 2000 Phase complete, 6100, 6101.

410. CORE PLUS PHASE (4000 PHASE)

1. General

a. The Core Plus Phase consists of academic, skill, and mission training.

b. Core Plus training is defined as theater specific and/or low likelihood of occurrence training and should not be the focus of unit training.

c. The Qualified Observer should be Core Skill complete prior to beginning the Core Plus Phase of training.

2. Core Plus Academics (ACAD)

ACAD-4000   2.0   *   B,R   CLRM   ASE Academics

General. At the publishing date of this manual, the ASE academic period of instruction is under development by the Syllabus Sponsor (VMR Det Belle Chase) and it will be distributed to the UC-12W community once completed.

ACAD-4001   4.0   730   B,R   CLRM   International

Goal. Qualified Observer under instruction is introduced to mission planning for extended over water and overseas operations.

Requirements. The QOUI will be introduced to mission planning for a multiday, long range flight that should include the crossing of international airspace. The following tools commonly used for mission planning in the international environment should be introduced: Optimum Path Aircraft Routing System (OPARS), Aircraft/Personnel Automated Clearance System (APACS), Foreign Clearance Guide, Area Planning/General Planning (AP/GP), Giant Report/Global Decision Support System 2 (GDSS2) account, Naval Flight Information Group (NavFIG), Jeppesen View and the validation and use of Jeppesen terminal approach procedures, Universal Flight Planning software for oceanic remote operations, North Atlantic/Pacific Tracks message, North Atlantic/Pacific Track Oceanic Checklist, North Atlantic/Pacific Minimum Navigation Performance Specification Airspace Operations Manual, Equal Time Point (ETP)/Point of No Return (PNR), and Aircraft Flight Manual (AFM) Supplement 63. The following contingency and emergency operations will also be discussed: engine failure (drift down), loss of pressurization, lost communication, and weather avoidance/contingency operations in an RVSM and or non radar environment.

Performance Standard. Successful completion of the course of instruction.

ACAD-4002   2.0   730   B,R   CLRM   MIL International

General. At the publishing date of this manual, the MIL International academic period of instruction is under development by the Syllabus Sponsor (VMR Det Belle Chase) and it will be distributed to the UC-12W community once completed.

3. Assault Support (AS). Operations that take place in a Low Threat (Permissive) environment and include specific procedures to minimize aircraft exposure to the threat. The procedures are designed to remain within the capabilities envelope of the aircraft and to maximize the protection capabilities of the ASE in the take-off and landing environment.

AS-4100   1.5   *   B,R   (N*)   A   1 UC-12W

General. At the publishing date of this manual, the AS flight is under development by the Syllabus Sponsor (VMR Det Belle Chase) and it will be distributed to the UC-12W community once approved.

Prerequisite. 4000

4. <u>Expeditionary Shore-Based Operations (EXP)</u>. Expeditionary operations are defined as operations to certified unimproved runways to include dirt, grass or gravel only.

EXP-4200   1.5* B,R   (N*)   A   1 UC-12W

> <u>Goal</u>. Conduct operations to certified unimproved runways to include dirt, gravel and grass.
>
> <u>Requirements</u>. Conduct aviation operations to certified unimproved runways in accordance with the limitations and guidelines in the NATOPS manual.
>
> Brief: The brief should include considerations for the specific type of runway to be used, including but not limited to: surface effects on runway length (takeoff, aborted takeoff, landing, etc). The following contingency and emergency operations will also be discussed: engine failure on take-off (before & after V1), single engine landing (specifically use of single engine reverse thrust), and abnormal flap configurations for landing.
>
> Conduct: QOUI to observe landings and takeoffs from certified unimproved runways (dirt, grass or gravel). A minimum of three normal T/O and landings to a full stop (no simulated emergency/abnormal conditions) are required for sortie completion.
>
> <u>Performance Standard</u>. Demonstrate competent knowledge of requirements for landing on unimproved runways.
>
> <u>Prerequisite</u>. 2000 Phase complete, 6100, 6101.

5. <u>International Procedures (INT)</u>

INT-4300   3.0   730 B,R   (N*)   A   1 UC-12W

> <u>Goal</u>. Qualified Observer under instruction performs extended range operations.
>
> <u>Requirement</u>. QOUI shall demonstrate the ability to assist the TAC with preflight preparation and managing a crew and aircraft away from home station on an operational mission that should include an RON.
>
> Brief: mission coordination, flight planning, weather, fuel planning, load computations, performance, CRM.
>
> Conduct: QOUI shall demonstrate excellent Crew Resource Management by assisting the TAC during an operational mission that includes a RON. During the trip, the QOUI shall assist in two-engine instrument approach.
>
> <u>Performance Standard</u>. Operate the aircraft according to the NFM IFM, FARs and ICAO procedures.
>
> <u>Prerequisite</u>. 4001

INT-4301   3.0   730 B,R   (N*)   A   1 UC-12W

> <u>Goal</u>. QOUI assists the TAC in conducting overwater navigation. Evaluation leg should be conducted with the QOUI demonstrating knowledge of all aspects of overwater flight.

Requirement. QOUI to demonstrate the ability to assist the TAC in managing a crew and aircraft on an extended, overwater flight under ICAO rules.

Brief: Mission coordination, crew briefing, ATFP briefing coordination, flight planning, weather brief, fuel planning, weight and balance, aircraft inspection, cargo inspection (as required), manifest inspection, trip aircraft clearance, foreign clearance guide review, survival gear inspection, fuel computations, performance, customs, and agriculture inspection.

Conduct: QOUI to conduct overwater navigation in accordance with ICAO, FAR and NATOPS convention. The following contingency and emergency operations will also be discussed: engine failure (drift down), loss of pressurization, lost communication, and weather avoidance/contingency operations in an RVSM and or non radar environment.

Performance Standard. Operate the aircraft according to the NFM IFM, FARs and ICAO procedures.

Prerequisite. 4001

411. REQUIREMENTS, QUALIFICATIONS, DESIGNATIONS (RQD) (6000 PHASE)

1. UC-12W RQD Academics

ACAD-6000   4.0   365   B,R   E   NATOPS Open Book

Goal. The open book examination shall consist of, but not be limited to the question bank. The purpose of the open book examination is to evaluate the Qualified Observer's knowledge of the appropriate publications and the aircraft.

Performance Standard. Achieve a minimum score of 3.5 on the open book examination.

ACAD-6001   2.0   365   B,R   E   NATOPS Closed Book

Goal. The purpose of the closed book examination is to evaluate the Qualified Observer's knowledge of normal/emergency procedures and aircraft limitations.

Performance Standard. Achieve a minimum score of 3.3 on the closed book examination.

Prerequisite. 6000

ACAD-6002   2.0   365   B,R   E   NATOPS Oral

Goal. The oral examination shall consist of, but not be limited to the question bank. The instructor may draw upon their experience to ask questions of a direct and objective nature to evaluate the Qualified Observer's knowledge of normal/emergency procedures, aircraft limitations, and performance.

Performance Standard. Achieve a minimum grade of qualified on the oral examination.

Prerequisite. 6000,6001

ACAD-6003   8.0   365   B,R   E   Instrument Ground School

Goal. The Instrument Ground School shall be an approved Commander Naval Air Forces (CNAF) syllabus. If an approved

Instrument Ground School is not available this requirement may be waived.

Performance Standard.   Achieve a minimum grade of qualified for Instrument Ground School.

ACAD-6004   2.0   365   B,R   E   Instrument Exam

Goal. Successful completion of the Instrument Examination.

Performance Standard. Achieve a minimum passing score on the Instrument Examination.

Prerequisite. 6003

ACAD-6005   2.0   365   B,R   E   Instrument Oral Exam

Goal. The oral NATOPS instrument examination shall consist of, but not be limited to the question bank in addition to any subject listed for coverage in OPNAVINST 3710.7.

Performance Standard. Achieve a minimum grade of qualified on the oral NATOPS instrument examination.

Prerequisite. 6004

ACAD-6006   1.0   365   B,R   E   CRM BASIC

Goal. Introduce Qualified Observer Crew Resource Management.

Requirement. This course of instruction is included in initial and Recurrent CACT.

ACAD-6007   1.0   365   B,R   E   CRM UC-12W

Goal. This course of instruction is under development by VMR Det Belle Chase, LA and will be distributed to the UC-12W community once completed.

ACAD-6009   1.0   30   B,R   E   Monthly EP Examination

Goal. Successfully complete the UC-12W Monthly Emergency Procedures Examination.

Requirement. Pass the Monthly Emergency Procedures Examination.

Performance Standard. Achieve a passing score on the Monthly Emergency Procedures Examination.

2. NATOPS Evaluation

NTPS-6100   2.0   365   B,R   (N*)   E   A/S   1 UC-12W/SIM

Goal. Complete annual NATOPS flight evaluation. Conduct an objective evaluation of the Qualified Observer's knowledge of mission planning, normal operating procedures (flight and ground), crew resource management, aircraft systems, performance criteria, emergency procedures, and debriefing. The focus is on normal and emergency procedures. Emphasis shall be placed on the aforementioned items with the addition of local course rules, unit SOP, and admin flight procedures. The NATOPS evaluation is intended to evaluate compliance with NATOPS procedures. The NATOPS evaluation is the means to measure the Qualified Observer's efficiency in the execution of normal operating procedures and reaction to emergencies and malfunctions. The NATOPS evaluation process should be as much a learning tool and/or experience as it is an evaluation.

Requirement. Demonstrate comprehensive knowledge and understanding of NATOPS, unit SOP, and local course rules.

Performance Standard. Executes flight and ground operations safely IAW OPNAV 3710.7, NATOPS and applicable manuals. Complies with unit SOP and local course rules.

Prerequisite. 6000, 6001, 6002.

NTPS-6103   .5   90   B,R   (N*) E   A   1 UC-12W (static)

Goal. Quarterly NATOPS static aircraft emergency procedures review.

Requirement. This review should cover selected aircraft emergencies in a static aircraft. This event can be completed in conjunction with a flight. Demonstrate comprehensive knowledge and understanding of NATOPS emergencies.

Performance Standard. Executes the review in accordance with NATOPS.

3. Transport Qualified Observer (QO)

QO-6500   1.5   365   B,R   D   E   A   1 UC-12W

Goal. QO evaluation flight.

Requirement. Demonstrate a thorough knowledge of the aircraft systems, the ability to perform the responsibilities of a QO and the ability to assist the TPC in all aircraft configurations under varying emergency and meteorological conditions.

Brief: Flight planning, weight and balance, fuel computations, knowledge and use of the Flight Management System (FMS) and normal and emergency procedures.

Flight: Demonstrate a proficiency in aircraft preflight, the use of all checklists, taxi & run-up procedures, radio and navigational operations, emergency procedures, shutdown checklists, and post flight.

Performance Standard. NFM.

Prerequisite. 2000 PHASE COMPLETE, 6000,6001,6300,6101,6103

412. AVIATION CAREER PROGRESSION MODEL (8000 PHASE)

1. Purpose

a. To enhance professional understanding of Marine Aviation and the MAGTF and ensure individuals possess the requisite skills to fill battle command and battle staff positions in support of the ACE and the MAGTF in a joint environment. The focus of training in the Aviation Career Progression Model (ACPM) is on academic events in the following areas:

Marine Air Command and Control System (MACCS)

Aviation Ground Support

Joint Air Operations

ACE Battle Staff

MAGTF

Seabased Operations

Combatant Commander Organizations

b. All tactical T/M/S T&R manuals have ACPM training requirements embedded within the progressive training phases, including the flight leadership POI. If not already completed prior to assignment to VMR-1 or a VMR det (C-9, UC-35, C-12, or C-20), Qualified Observers assigned to an OSA platform shall complete ACPM training requirements as outlined per their original T/M/S MOS T&R manual. Refer to NAVMC 3500.14, Aviation T&R Program Manual, as a primary reference for ACPM training requirements.

2. General

a. The ACPM is intended to be an integrated series of academic events contained within each phase of training. Accordingly, ACPM academic events are like any other academic event in that they serve as pre-requisites to selected flight events or stages. Additionally, several ACPM academic events are integrated as prerequisites for flight leadership syllabi.

b. ACPM academic events, along with their identifying prerequisite association with other training phases/stages/events are listed below.

VMR-1 VMR Det (UC-12W)				
ACPM TO UC-12W T&R MATRIX				
STAGE	EVENT NUMBER	CLASS	ACPM DESCRIPTION	PREREQUISITE TO (PHASE/STAGE/EVENT)
ACPM	8200	(U)	MACCS AGENCIES, FUNCTIONS AND CONTROL OF AIRCRAFT AND MISSLES	2000 PHASE
ACPM	8201	(U)	MWCS BRIEF	2000 PHASE
ACPM	8202	(U)	ACA AND AIRSPACE	2000 PHASE
ACPM	8210	(U)	AVIATION GROUND SUPPORT	2000 PHASE
ACPM	8230	(U)	ACE BATTLESTAFF	2000 PHASE
ACPM	8231	(U)	BATTLE COMMAND DISPLAY	2000 PHASE
ACPM	8240	(U)	SIX FUNCTIONS OF MARINE AVIATION	2000 PHASE
ACPM	8241	(U)	JTAR/ASR INTRODUCTION AND PRACTICAL APPLICATION CLASS	2000 PHASE
ACPM	8242	(U)	SITE COMMAND PRIMER	2000 PHASE
ACPM	8250	(U)	THEATER AIR GROUND SYSTEM (TAGS)	2000 PHASE
ACPM	8300	(U)	AIR DEFENSE	3000 PHASE
ACPM	8310	(U)	FORWARD ARMING AND REFUELING POINT (FARP) OPERATIONS	3000 PHASE
ACPM	8311	(U)	MARINE CORPS TACTICAL FUEL SYSTEMS	3000 PHASE
ACPM	8320	(U)	JOINT STRUCTURE & JOINT AIR OPERATIONS	3000 PHASE
ACPM	8321	(U)	JOINT AIR TASKING CYCLE PHASE 1: STRATEGY DEVELOPMENT	3000 PHASE
ACPM	8322	(U)	JOINT AIR TASKING CYCLE PHASE 2: TARGET DEVELOPMENT	3000 PHASE
ACPM	8323	(U)	JOINT AIR TASKING CYCLE PHASE 3: WEAPONING AND ALLOCATION	3000 PHASE
ACPM	8324	(U)	JOINT AIR TASKING CYCLE PHASE 4: JOINT ATO PRODUCTION	3000 PHASE
ACPM	8325	(U)	JOINT AIR TASKING CYCLE PHASE 5:	3000 PHASE
ACPM	8326	(U)	JOINT AIR TASKING CYCLE PHASE 6: COMBAT ASSESSMENT	3000 PHASE
ACPM	8340	(U)	INTEGRATING FIRES AND AIRSPACE WITHIN THE MAGTF	3000 PHASE
ACPM	8350	(U)	PHASING CONTROL ASHORE	3000 PHASE
ACPM	8351	(U)	TACRON ORGANIZATIONS AND FUNCTIONS	3000 PHASE
ACPM	8630	(U)	TACTICAL AIR COMMAND CENTER (TACC)	6000 PHASE
ACPM	8660	(U)	JOINT OPS INTRO	6000 PHASE

Enclosure (1)

ACPM	8640	(U)	JOINT DATA NETWORK	6000 PHASE
ACPM	8641	(U)	MAGTF THEATER	6000 PHASE
ACPM	8620	(U)	ESG/CSG INTEGRATION	6000 PHASE

413. UC-12W T&R SYLLABUS MATRIX

UC-12W QUALIFIED OBSERVER (QO) T&R MATRIX

STAGE	TRNG CODE	T&R DESCRIPTION	POI	E	DEVICE	# OF A/C	CON	RE FLY	# OF ACAD	ACAD TIME	# OF SIM	SIM TIME	# OF FLTS	FLT TIME	PREREQUISITE	NOTES	CHAINING	EVENT CONV
		CORE SKILL INTRODUCTION TRAINING (1000 PHASE EVENTS)																
		CORE SKILL ACADEMICS																
ACAD	1000	CACT GND SCHL INITIAL	B					*		48.0								
ACAD	1001	CACT GND SCHL REFRESH	B					365		8.0					1000			
ACAD	1002	RVSM	B					*		3.0								
ACAD	1003	WEATHER RADAR	B,R					365		2.0								
ACAD	1004	CACT INTERNATIONAL PROCEDURES INITIAL	B,R					*		21.0								
ACAD	1005	CACT INTERNATIONAL PROCEDURES RECURRENT	R					730		8.0					1004			
		ACAD TOTAL							6	90.0	0	0.0	0	0.0				
		COMMAND AIRCRAFT CREW TRAINING (CACT)																
CACT	1101	CACT SIM 1	B		S		(N*)	*				4.0						
CACT	1102	CACT SIM 2	B		S		(N*)	*				4.0						
CACT	1103	CACT SIM 3	B		S		(N*)	*				4.0						
CACT	1104	CACT SIM 4	B		S		(N*)	*				4.0						
CACT	1105	CACT SIM 5	B,R		S		(N*)	365				4.0						
CACT	1106	CACT SIM 6	B,R		S		(N*)	365				4.0						
CACT	1107	CACT SIM 7	B,R		S		(N*)	365				4.0						
		CACT INT SIM TOTAL							0	0.0	7	28.0	0	0.0				
		CORE SKILL INTRODUCTION TRAINING (1000 PHASE EVENTS) TOTAL							6	90.0	7	28.0	0	0.0				
		CORE SKILL TRAINING (2000 PHASE)																
		CORE SKILL ACADEMICS (ACAD)																
ACAD	2000	INTRO LOCAL PROC	B,R				D	*		3.0					1000, 1001, CACT COMP, 1107			
ACAD	2001	FMS PROCEDURES	B,R				D	*		3.0					2000			
		TOTAL ACAD STAGE							2	6.0	0	0.0	0	0.0				
		FAMILIARIZATION (FAM)																
FAM	2100	INTRO UC-12W A/C	B		A	1	D	*						2.0	2000,2001			
FAM	2101	INTRO EXPANDED	B,R		A	1	D	365						2.0	2100			

UC-12W QUALIFIED OBSERVER (QO) T&R MATRIX

STAGE	TRNG CODE	T&R DESCRIPTION	POI	E	DEVICE	# OF A/C	CON	RE FLY	# OF ACAD	ACAD TIME	# OF SIM	SIM TIME	# OF FLTS	FLT TIME	PREREQUISITE	NOTES	CHAINING	EVENT CONV
		ENVELOPE																
		TOTAL FAM STAGE							0	0.0	0	0.0	2	4.0				
		INSTRUMENTS (INST)																
INST	2200	INTRO INST NAV	B,R		A	1	(N*)	*						2.0	2101			
INST	2201	HIGH ALT OPS	B,R		A	1	(N*)	365						2.0	2101			
		TOTAL INST STAGE							0	0.0	0	0.0	2	4.0				
		CORE SKILL TRAINING (2000 PHASE EVENTS) TOTAL							2	6.0	0	0.0	4	8.0				
		MISSION SKILL TRAINING (3000 PHASE)																
		OPERATIONAL SUPPORT AIRLIFT (OSA)																
OSA	3100	OSA	B,R		A	1	(N*)	60						2.0	2000 PHASE COMPLETE, 6100, 6101	PAX	2201,3200	
		TOTAL OSA STAGE							0	0.0	0	0.0	1	2.0				
		AIR LOGISTICS SUPPORT (ALS)																
ALS	3200	ALS	B,R		A	1	(N*)	60						2.0	2000 PHASE COMPLETE, 6100, 6101	CARGO	2201,3100	
		TOTAL ALS STAGE							0	0.0	0	0.0	1	2.0				
		TOTAL MISSION SKILL TRAINING (3000 PHASE EVENTS)							0	0.0	0	0.0	2	4.0				
		CORE PLUS TRAINING (4000 PHASE)																
		CORE PLUS ACADEMICS																
ACAD	4000	ASE Academics	B,R							2.0								
ACAD	4001	CACT International Procedures	B,R					730		4.0								
ACAD	4002	Military International Procedures	B,R					730		2.0					1002			
		TOTAL ACAD STAGE							3	8.0	0								
		ASSAULT SUPPORT (AS)																
AS	4100	ASE Procedures	B,R		A	1	D	730						2.0	4000	ASE	3100,3200	
		TOTAL AS STAGE							0	0.0	0	0.0	1	2.0				

UC-12W QUALIFIED OBSERVER (QO) T&R MATRIX

STAGE	TRNG CODE	T&R DESCRIPTION	POI	DEVICE E	DEVICE A	# OF A/C	CON	RE FLY	# OF ACAD	ACAD TIME	# OF SIM	SIM TIME	# OF FLTS	FLT TIME	PREREQUISITE	NOTES	CHAINING	EVENT CONV
EXPEDITIONARY SHORE-BASED OPERATIONS (EXP)																		
EXP	4200	Unimproved Runway Operations	B,R		A	1	(N*)	*	0	0	0	0.0	1	2.0	2000 PHASE Complete, 6100, 6101		3100, 3200	
		TOTAL EXP STAGE							0	0	0	0.0	1	2.0				
INTERNATIONAL PROCEDURES (INT)																		
INT	4300	INTL OSA	B,R		A	1	(N*)	730	0		0		3	3.0	4001		3100,3200,2201,4301,4100	
INT	4301	INTL ALS	B,R		A	1	(N*)	730	0		0		3	3.0	4001		3100,3200,2201,4300,4100	
		TOTAL INT STAGE							0		0	0.0	6	6.0				
		CORE PLUS TRAINING (3000 PHASE EVENTS) TOTAL							3	8.0	0	0.0	4	10.0				
		1000, 2000, 3000, & 4000 PHASE TOTAL							11	104	7	28.0	12	28.5				
REQUIREMENT, QUALIFICATIONS, AND DESIGNATIONS (RQD) (6000 PHASE)																		
RQD ACADEMICS (ACAD)																		
ACAD	6000	NATOPS Open Book Exam	B,R	E				365		4.0								
ACAD	6001	NATOPS Closed Book Exam	B,R	E				365		2.0					6000			
ACAD	6002	NATOPS Oral Exam	B,R	E				365		2.0					6000, 6001			
ACAD	6003	Instrument Ground School	B,R	E				365		8.0								
ACAD	6004	Instrument Exam	B,R	E				365		2.0					6003			
ACAD	6005	Instrument Oral Exam	B,R	E				365		2.0					6004			
ACAD	6006	CRM BASIC	B,R	E				365		1.0								
ACAD	6007	CRM T/M/S	B,R	E				365		1.0								
ACAD	6009	Monthly EP Exam	B,R	E				30		1.0								
		TOTAL ACAD STAGE							9	23.0	0	0.0	0	0.0				
NATOPS																		
NATOPS	6100	NATOPS Evaluation	B,R	E	A/S	1	(N*)	365						2.0	6000,6001,6002,2000 Phase Complete, 8200-8250	STATIC A/C		
NATOPS	6103	Quarterly EP Eval	B,R	E	A		(N*)	90						0.0				
		NATOPS TOTAL							0	0.0	0	0.0	2	2.0				
TRANSPORT QUALIFIED OBSERVER (QO)																		
T2P	6500	T2P UPGRADE	B,R	E	A	1	D	365	0	0.0	0	0.0	1	1.5	2000 Phase complete, 6101, 6103			
		TOTAL T2P STAGE							0	0.0	0	0.0	1	1.5				

UC-12W QUALIFIED OBSERVER (QO) T&R MATRIX

STAGE	TRNG CODE	T&R DESCRIPTION	POI	E	DEVICE	# OF A/C	CON	RE FLY	# OF ACAD	ACAD TIME	# OF SIM	SIM TIME	# OF FLTS	FLT TIME	PREREQUISITE	NOTES	CHAINING	EVENT CONV
		AVIATION CAREER PROGRESSION MODEL (ACPM)																
ACPM	8200	MACCS AGENCIES, FUNCTIONS AND CONTROL OF AIRCRAFT AND MISSLES						*		0.5					2000 PHASE			
ACPM	8201	MWCS BRIEF						*		0.4					2000 PHASE			
ACPM	8202	ACA AND AIRSPACE						*		0.5					2000 PHASE			
ACPM	8210	AVIATION GROUND SUPPORT						*		0.6					2000 PHASE			
ACPM	8230	ACE BATTLESTAFF BATTLE COMMAND						*		0.6					2000 PHASE			
ACPM	8231	DISPLAY						*		0.3					2000 PHASE			
ACPM	8240	SIX FUNCTIONS OF MARINE AVIATION						*		1.3					2000 PHASE			
ACPM	8241	JTAR/ASR INTRODUCTION AND PRACTICAL APPLICATION CLASS						*		0.5					2000 PHASE			
ACPM	8242	SITE COMMAND PRIMER						*		0.7					2000 PHASE			
ACPM	8250	THEATER AIR GROUND SYSTEM (TAGS)						*		0.6					2000 PHASE			
ACPM	8300	AIR DEFENSE						*		0.6					3000 PHASE			
ACPM	8310	FORWARD ARMING AND REFUELING POINT (FARP) OPERATIONS						*		0.4					3000 PHASE			
ACPM	8311	MARINE CORPS TACTICAL FUEL SYSTEMS						*		0.2					3000 PHASE			
ACPM	8320	JOINT STRUCTURE & JOINT AIR OPERATIONS						*		1.3					3000 PHASE			
ACPM	8321	JOINT AIR TASKING CYCLE PHASE 1: STRATEGY DEVELOPMENT						*		0.3					3000 PHASE			
ACPM	8322	JOINT AIR TASKING CYCLE PHASE 2: TARGET DEVELOPMENT						*		0.2					3000 PHASE			
ACPM	8323	JOINT AIR TASKING CYCLE PHASE 3: WEAPONING AND ALLOCATION						*		0.2					3000 PHASE			

Enclosure (1)

UC-12W QUALIFIED OBSERVER (QO) T&R MATRIX

STAGE	TRNG CODE	T&R DESCRIPTION	POI	E	DEVICE	# OF A/C	CON	RE FLY	# OF ACAD	ACAD TIME	# OF SIM	SIM TIME	# OF FLTS	FLT TIME	PREREQUISITE	NOTES	CHAINING	EVENT CONV
ACPM	8324	JOINT AIR TASKING CYCLE PHASE 4: JOINT ATO PRODUCTION						*		0.2					3000 PHASE			
ACPM	8325	JOINT AIR TASKING CYCLE PHASE 5:						*		0.2					3000 PHASE			
ACPM	8326	JOINT AIR TASKING CYCLE PHASE 6: COMBAT ASSESMENT						*		0.2					3000 PHASE			
ACPM	8340	INTEGRATING FIRES AND AIRSPACE WITHIN THE MAGTF						*		0.5					3000 PHASE			
ACPM	8350	PHASING CONTROL ASHORE						*		0.5					3000 PHASE			
ACPM	8351	TACRON ORGANIZATIONS AND FUNCTIONS						*		TBD					3000 PHASE			
ACPM	8630	TACTICAL AIR COMMAND CENTER (TACC)						*		0.7					6000 PHASE			
ACPM	8660	JOINT OPS INTRO						*		0.4					6000 PHASE			
ACPM	8640	JOINT DATA NETWORK						*		0.4					6000 PHASE			
ACPM	8641	MAGTF THEATER						*		1.5					6000 PHASE			
ACPM	8620	ESG/CSG INTEGRATION						*		TBD					6000 PHASE			
		TOTAL ACPM STAGE							28	13.9	0	0.0	0	0.0				

414.   DC/A LETTER 17 MAY 2010; REMOVAL OF NFO WAIVER OPTION

DEPARTMENT OF THE NAVY
HEADQUARTERS UNITED STATES MARINE CORPS
3000 MARINE CORPS PENTAGON
WASHINGTON, DC 20350-3000

IN REPLY REFER TO:

3710
AVN
17 May 2010

From: Deputy Commandant for Aviation, United States Marine Corps
To: Chief of Naval Operations, Code OPNAV N88
      Commander Naval Air Systems Command; Code Air 4.0P
      Chief of Naval Air Training, Code 00
      Commander, U.S. Marine Corps Forces Command, Code DOSS, G3
      Commander, U.S. Marine Forces Pacific, Code DOSS, G3
      Commander, Naval Reserve Forces Command, Code 00
      Commanding General, 4th Marine Aircraft Wing, Code DOSS, G3
      Commander, Naval Safety Center, Code 00
      Chief, Bureau of Medicine and Surgery, Code NAMI, ASTI

Subj: REMOVAL OF NFO WAIVER OPTION FROM UC-12B/F/W NATOPS

1.   I have been briefed on the issue of UC-12 NATOPS waivers for
USMC NFO aircrew, a program that has served the Marine Corps well
over many years. I do not support a change to OPNAV 3710.7, UC-
12 NATOPS, or the UC-12 T&R syllabus that will eliminate the NFO
Waiver or Qualified Observer syllabus.

2.   The Navy may elect to strike the NFO Waiver for its VR/OSA
units, leaving the Marine Corps the option to utilize the waiver.
It is essential that the NFO waiver remain available to Marine
Aviation in order to support USMC UC-12 unit missions.

3.   Given the solid safety record over the years of USMC NFO's
in UC-12 aircraft, there is no cause to remove the waiver as an
interim or permanent change to the NATOPS Flight Manual or UC-12
Training & Readiness (T&R) Manual. Retention of the waiver
provides Marine Corps Aviation flexibility in staffing through
2025. Utilization of the NFO waiver shall be used wisely to
support OSA missions.

GEORGE J. TRAUTMAN III

Copy to:
Commander, Fleet Logistics Support Wing, Code 00

415.   DC/A MSG 101812Z JUN 10 USMC UC-12BFW NFO-QO WAIVER

USMC UC-12BFW NAVAL FLIGHT OFFICER-QUALIFIED OBSERVER (NFO-QO)
WAIVER RETENTION AND TASKS

DTG: 101812Z Jun 10
Precedence: ROUTINE
DAC: General
To: CMC WASHINGTON DC I(UC), CMC WASHINGTON DC L LF(UC), CMC WASHINGTON
DC MRA MP(UC), CMC WASHINGTON DC MRA(UC), CMC WASHINGTON DC PPO(UC),
COMMARFORCOM ALD(UC), COMMARFORCOM G-1(UC), COMMARFORCOM G3-5-7(UC),
COMMARFORCOM(UC), CG MCIEAST(UC), MCAS NEW RIVER NC(UC), HHS MCAS
BEAUFORT SC(UC), HHS MCAS NEW RIVER NC(UC), COMMARFORPAC ALD(UC),
COMMARFORPAC G1(UC), COMMARFORPAC G3(UC), COMMARFORPAC(UC), CG MCI
WEST(UC), CO MCAS MIRAMAR CA(UC), HHS MCAS MIRAMAR CA(UC), HHS MCAS
YUMA AZ(UC), CG MCB CAMP BUTLER JP(UC), MCAS IWAKUNI JP(UC), MCAS YUMA
AZ(UC), MCAS FUTENMA JP(UC), HHS MCAS FUTENMA JP(UC), COMMARFORRES
G1(UC), COMMARFORRES G3(UC), COMMARFORRES(UC), CG 4TH MAW ALD(UC), CG
4TH MAW G1(UC), CG 4TH MAW G3(UC), CG MCCDC QUANTICO VA(UC), CG TECOM
ATB(UC), CNO WASHINGTON DC(UC), COMNAVAIRFOR SAN DIEGO CA,
COMNAVAIRFORES SAN DIEGO CA(UC), COMNAVAIRSYSCOM PATUXENT RIVER MD(UC),
CMC WASHINGTON DC AVN APW(UC), CMC WASHINGTON DC AVN ASL(UC), CMC
WASHINGTON DC AVN ASM(UC), CMC WASHINGTON DC AVN(UC), CMC WASHINGTON DC
AVN APC(UC), CMC WASHINGTON DC AVN APP(UC), COMNAVFACENGCOM WASHINGTON
DC(UC), COMFLELOGSUPPWING FORT WORTH TX(UC), BUMED WASHINGTON DC(UC),
VMR DET ANDREWS(UC), VMR DET NEW ORLEANS(UC)

UNCLASSIFIED//
MSGID/GENADMIN/CMC WASHINGTON DC AVN//
SUBJ/USMC UC-12BFW NAVAL FLIGHT OFFICER-QUALIFIED OBSERVER (NFO-QO)
WAIVER RETENTION AND TASKS//
REF/A/MSGID: LTR/HQMC DC AVN 3710 17 MAY 2010// REF/B/OPNAV3710.7U//
REF/C/A1-C12BM-NFM-00 NATOPS FLIGHT MANUAL NAVY MODEL UC-12BFM
AIRCRAFT// REF/D/ NAVMC 3500.30 UC-12 TRAINING & READINESS MANUAL//
AMPN/REF A IS DC AVIATION LETTER STATING INTENT TO RETAIN UC-12 NFO-QO
WAIVER FOR USMC AVIATION UNITS// REF B IS OPNAV INSTRUCTION 3710.7U
NATOPS GENERAL FLIGHT AND OPERATING INSTRUCTIONS//REF C IS THE UC-
12B/F/M NATOPS FLIGHT MANUAL//REF D IS THE USMC UC-12 TRAINING &
READINESS MANUAL// POC/HOUDE, R.J./CTR/APP-48/-/TEL:703-693-8539/EMAIL:
ROBERT.HOUDE.CTR@USMC.MIL//
GENTEXT/REMARKS//
1. PER REF A, DEPUTY COMMANDANT FOR AVIATION (DC AVN) STATED INTENT IS
TO MAINTAIN OR INCLUDE NFO-QO COPILOT WAIVER IN ALL UC-12 TMS NATOPS
FLIGHT MANUALS (NFM). SPECIFIC GUIDANCE FOLLOWS, WHICH SUPPORTS USMC
USE OF NFO-QO IN THE PERFORMANCE OF COPILOT DUTIES FOR TRANSPORT
MISSIONS.
2. NFO-QO ISSUE HAS GENERATED DISCUSSION CONCERNING INTERPRETATION OF
OPNAV 3710.7U AND UC-12 NATOPS FLIGHT MANUAL (NFM). NAVAL SAFETY
CENTER UC-12 DATA ANALYSIS CONTAINS NO HAZREP OR MISHAP CAUSAL OR
CONTRIBUTING FACTORS ATTRIBUTABLE TO NFOS ACTING AS COPILOTS IN UC-12
AIRCRAFT. HISTORIC PERFORMANCE OF USMC NFOS ACTING AS COPILOT IN
CONDUCT OF TRANSPORT MISSIONS, CLEARLY DEMONSTRATES THAT PROPERLY
TRAINED AND QUALIFIED NFOS PROVIDE USMC OSA UNIT COMMANDING OFFICERS

Enclosure (1)

WITH AIRCREW FULLY CAPABLE OF EXECUTING OSA TRANSPORT MISSIONS IN UC-12 AIRCRAFT.

3. HQMC SERVICE POSITION.

A. REF B STATES "THE MINIMUM FLIGHT CREW REQUIREMENTS FOR NAVAL AIRCRAFT ARE SET FORTH IN THE APPLICABLE NATOPS MANUAL FOR INDIVIDUAL AIRCRAFT MODELS." THE UC-12B/F/M NFM HAS CLEAR GUIDANCE DEFINING THE MINIMUM FLIGHT CREW NECESSARY FOR TRAINING, POST-MAINTENANCE FUNCTIONAL CHECK FLIGHT, AND TRANSPORT MISSIONS.

B. COMMANDER FLEET LOGISTICS SUPPORT WING (CFLSW) JRB FT. WORTH IS UC-12B/F/M MODEL MANAGER. CFLSW PROPOSED AN INTERIM NATOPS CHANGE TO REMOVE NFO-QO FROM REF C, WHICH STATES "WHEN A QUALIFIED NFO IS ASSIGNED AS COPILOT, HIS/HER DUTIES ARE THE SAME AS LISTED BELOW, EXCEPT HE/SHE SHALL NOT ASSUME PHYSICAL CONTROL OF THE AIRCRAFT."

B.1. DC AVN DOES NOT SUPPORT REMOVAL OF NFO-QO FROM REF C. NAVY MAY REMOVE THE NFO-QO OPTION FOR ITS VR/OSA UNITS, USMC SHALL RETAIN NFO-QO WAIVER.

B.2. NFO-QO RISK MANAGEMENT AND MITIGATION CONTROLS ARE IN PLACE TO ADDRESS SAFE UC-12 MISSION OPERATIONS. PRECEDENCE AND PAST PERFORMANCE OF NFOS ACTING AS COPILOTS WARRANT THE RETENTION OF THE NFO-QO WAIVER FOR THE UC-12B/F/M NFM FOR USMC NFOS.

C. THE UC-12W NFM IS CURRENTLY IN "DRAFT." IT SHALL INCLUDE THE SAME SUPPORTING LANGUAGE THE UC-12B/F/M NFM HAS CURRENTLY REGARDING THE NFO-QO CREW POSITION. THIS ACTION SUPPORTS COMMANDING OFFICERS WITH PROPERLY TRAINED AIRCREW TO FULLY EXECUTE TRANSPORT MISSIONS, AS CURRENTLY DEFINED.

D. IN THE FUTURE, WHEN INCREASED CAPABILITIES ARE ADDED TO THE UC-12W, THE ROLE OF THE COPILOT (SPECIFICALLY NFO-QO) WILL BE RE-EVALUATED IN SUPPORT OF THOSE ADDITIONAL WARFIGHTING CAPABILITIES ADDED TO THESE AIRCRAFT PLATFORMS.

4. TASKS.

A. FOR COMMANDER FLEET LOGISTICS SUPPORT WING UC-12B/F/M NATOPS PROGRAM MANAGER: RETAIN NFO WAIVER LANGUAGE FOR USMC NFOS IN UC-12B/F/M NFM.

B. FOR UC-12W MODEL MANAGER (VMR DET BELLE CHASSE, LA.):

1) ENSURE NFO-QO WAIVER LANGUAGE, CREW DESCRIPTION, CREW QUALIFICATION AND CHECKLISTS FOR USMC UC-12W NFO-QO IS INCLUDED IN ALL UC-12W NATOPS PUBLICATIONS AS APPLICABLE.

2) ENSURE LANGUAGE MATCHES THAT FOUND IN THE UC-12B/F/M NFM.

3) ENSURE NFO-QO SYLLABUS IS INCLUDED IN REF D FOR ALL USMC UC-12 TRAINING & READINESS MANUALS AS APPROPRIATE.

C. FOR HQMC AVIATION PLANS & POLICY (APP) AND AVIATION WEAPON SYSTEM REQUIREMENTS (APW) BRANCHES: SUBMIT INTERIM CHANGE TO OPNAV 3710.7U TO INCLUDE LANGUAGE WHICH SUPPORTS USMC NFO-QO UC-12 COPILOT POSITION. LANGUAGE WILL CLARIFY NFO WAIVER AND SUPPORT UC-12 MODEL MANAGERS IN EXECUTION OF THEIR DUTIES.

5. POCS:

A. POC/NELSON, T.M./COL/APP-B1/TEL:703-693-8553DSN 223/ EMAIL: THOMAS.M.NELSON@USMC.MIL//

B. POC/HOUDE, R./CTR/APP-48/TEL:703-693-8539DSN 223/ EMAIL: ROBERT.HOUDE.CTR@USMC.MIL //

C. POC/GIERBER, G/CTR/APW-71A/TEL:703-693-8451DSN 223/ EMAIL: GUSTAVO.GIERBER1.CTR@USMC.MIL.//